BIG TREES
of NORTHERN NEW ENGLAND

Short Hikes *to the* Biggest Trees *in*
Northern Massachusetts, Vermont,
New Hampshire *and* Maine

by KEVIN MARTIN

T0269976

Peter E. Randall Publisher
Portsmouth, New Hampshire
2022

ISBN: 978-1-937721-87-9
Library of Congress Control Number: 2022911022

Published by
Jetty House, an imprint of
Peter E. Randall Publisher LLC
5 Greenleaf Woods Drive, U102
Portsmouth, NH 03801
www.perpublisher.com

Book design: Grace Peirce

Additional copies available from:
Kevin Martin
16 Windsor Lane
Epping, NH 03042
Email: kevinmartin16@comcast.net

Map sources:
Maine and Vermont maps courtesy of QGIS 3.24, an open-source GIS licensed
under the GNU General Public License, a project of the Open Source Geospacial
Foundation. Find on the web at www.qgis.org.
New Hampshire maps courtesy of NH Granit, New Hampshire's statewide GIS
clearinghouse: www.granit.unh.edu.
Massachusetts maps courtesy of Massmapper – Mass GIS (Bureau of Geographic
Information), Commonwealth of Massachusetts EOTSS: www.massgis.gov.

Photographs by Kevin Martin unless otherwise noted.
Printed in the United States of America

Contents

Acknowledgments

I would like to first acknowledge the help of those in charge of the Big Tree Programs in the four states with trees showing in this book.

In New Hampshire, Mary Tebo Davis keeps the program going and, along with Mary Jane Sheldon, has ensured that the extensive database of trees is kept up to date. I used that database to research which trees were available for the public to see. John Wallace, the current state coordinator, has allowed me to research whatever info I needed to show off the trees in the state. Sam Stoddard, Fred Borman, Dode Gladders, Greg Jordan, Dave Govatski, and other current and retired foresters helped with any questions about tree ID or features that I could include. Brian Beaty, former arborist for the Dartmouth College Campus, and William Nichols, New Hampshire state botanist, also chipped in.

In Maine, Jan Ames Santerre is in charge of the Big Tree Program. Jan helped by supplying info on trees on public land and showed me some in the Portland area. The previous Big Tree expert, Fred Huntress, was also helpful in telling me where to look for trees. Oxford County retired forester Merl Ring showed me some in his county and supplied a pamphlet they had put together on the biggest trees there. Patty Cormier, the current state forester, took me on a long daytrip climbing a mountain, measuring a few trees, and putting out a fire. Dave Tibbets of the US Fish and Wildlife Service pointed out several trees he noticed while surveying the AT and other lands in Maine.

In Vermont, Jeffrey Freeman, who was the former Big Tree specialist for that state, supplied a booklet he put out telling about the trees in Vermont and where they are located. He then showed me some in the town of Rutland. Danielle Fitzko, the most recent state coordinator for the program, fielded some of my questions. Now-retired foresters Richard Greenwood and Bill Guenther were particularly helpful. Jason Bedard of the Upper Valley Land Trust showed off one of their protected properties. Foresters Cory Creagan and Jim White helped with the Fisher Scott trees and the history of the family that donated that land. Vermont's many town tree wardens also helped by directing me to trees and answering questions. As of 2022, Gwen Kozslowski of the Urban and Community Forestry Program has been updating the Big Tree listings. Thanks to Tim Terway of the Vermont Center for Geographical Information for helping to navigate the GIS map system in Vermont.

In Massachusetts, Ken Gooch of the Big Tree Registry answered some of my early questions in that state. State foresters Julie Coop and Mollie Freilicher of the Urban and Community Forest Program keep track of the legacy trees and helped by supplying tree lists and directing me on how to go forward in that state. The Massachusetts Audubon Society directed me to trees on the many properties they manage. Robert Leverett, a Big Tree and old-growth expert, helped keep me up to date on proper measuring methods to meet the National Big Tree Program requirements.

Many other foresters, arborists, botanists, tree wardens, land trust workers, cemetery managers, and others were instrumental in helping me find and measure the trees throughout the four states. I appreciate their willingness to help with the project.

Last but not least, my family, who put up with several years of Big Tree searching and did not roll their eyes much until the last few years. My wife, Kim, travelled with me to many parts of northern New England, with my brothers, children, and grandchildren taking trips at times. Love and thanks to them all. I hope they enjoyed the visits and will remember and revisit the trees when they find the need.

Sponsors

I would like to acknowledge support for this book from Goosebay Lumber and Sawmill in Chichester, NH. They are family-owned and operated since 1978, stocking over 70 species of hardwood and specialty softwood, much of it sourced locally. They supply lumber for the many woodworkers in northern New England and have a sawmill operation that helps support the local loggers. Be sure to check them out for your lumber needs.

Thanks also to Jerry Langdon for his support. He is a board member of the NH Tree Farm Program and helps his son run the Twin Pines Golf Driving Range in Epping, NH.

Introduction

We all seem attracted to large trees, especially when they are deep in the forest and stand out among the other trees near them. It feels like you are in a different world when under the tree and looking out from the space that is carved out by the limbs. The bark is more noticeable, as it has a look and feel that draws you in closer to examine it. If it is a tall tree, the trunk goes up and up and you strain to see the top, while the shorter giants have stout lower branches that look like a regular-sized tree growing sideways out of the trunk. Most locals who use the woods will know where you are directing them, when you say "over by the big oak." You can sit under it and let your mind wander, feeling protected by this old forest landmark that has had generations of landowners, hunters, fisherman, and hikers stop for a while to ease the stress of their busy lives.

This book will direct you to an assortment of large trees in northern New England that take a little hike to get to. I tried to include some from most parts of region so you can travel to different types of forests and see new things on the way. The North Country has its tamarack, spruce-fir, northern white cedar, and beech-birch hardwood forests that are in the furthest and wildest reaches of the region. The mountains south to the Lakes regions have a mix of the more northern forest species, like the spruce and fir, along with some oaks and pines. The coast and valleys along the Big Rivers in the more southern regions have the oak, pine, and hickory woods that I know best. These trips will take you into deep swamps, along the river edges and floodplains, into some mountains with their valleys, and down in the flatland near the ocean. The cities and towns of the area have many of the largest Big Trees, as they are well cared for, have plenty of sunlight, and little or no competition from other trees. Some of the trips are into these cities or towns where there are several trees that you can walk or bike to and view from the sidewalks.

In today's society, with so many distractions bringing us inside and out of the elements, it is important to be reminded of the natural world and the trees around us. These large plants do so much to keep our world in balance. They help control flooding by absorbing water and prevent erosion during heavy rains. They absorb much of the carbon we introduce into the air and give us the oxygen we breathe. Viewing these larger trees will help us appreciate the tremendous work that they do. We use them in many ways, such as building and furnishing our homes, as a source of heat, and even to cure our illnesses. This book tries to showcase different types of the Big Trees, so if you do not already know some of the species, you can learn to ID them. There may be more than one impressive example of the more common trees, as some just have to be seen.

While the guidebook is up to date as of 2022, keep in mind that the Big Tree Champions list is always changing. The big trees in the state listings are supposed to be updated every ten years, but as with many volunteer organizations, it does not always happen. When they do get checked, a common occurrence when searching them out is that the tree has been cut, blown over, or just died and rotted from old age or disease. I have learned not to be too discouraged when you find the trees like that. It is just the way it is, and another younger tree is always willing to try to reach the grand stature the old giant had attained. Some of the hikes in this book include trees that are not state or county champions, although they may have been at one time until a larger one was found and the former champ moved down on the list. They are still impressive trees and include a nice hike to get to them.

My hope is that this book will draw attention and support for the Big Trees and forestlands in the area. Enjoy and be sure to look around while out in the woods of northern New England!

What You Will Need to Bring

- Water
- Snacks
- Warm clothing- if needed
- Compass
- Boots for wet areas
- Tree measuring gear – if desired
- Binoculars
- Tree ID book
- Camera
- Map of area
- Insect repellent
- GPS – needed to find most of the trees

For the longer hikes, you should bring many items you would normally take hiking. I keep a bag with necessities in it for just such hikes. Even some of the shorter hikes are in woods that are hard to get around in; be prepared with a GPS (with extra batteries) and a map and compass for backup. During hunting season, be sure to wear some hunter's orange clothing to be safe.

Always respect the property you are on and the trees you are viewing. Do not let the kids pull off the bark or hack away at the trunk with whatever they have in hand. Tread softly around the tree and try not to damage any exposed roots. Don't hug them if you see the ground getting compacted around the roots, just get close enough to appreciate their size then stand back for a better look.

Some trees are on private property, and it could be posted at any time if owners change or the land is abused. If the land is posted, move on to see another tree. If in a city and an owner is kind enough to let us view the tree, be kind enough to respect their privacy and do not hang around the front of their house too long. If they want, they will come to you and tell you about the tree, but they may not want too many people asking a lot of questions. Even trees on public land will be protected if abused, and steps could be taken to restrict viewing them. Just use some common sense and our children may bring the grandchildren back to see the same trees in the future.

Trip Difficulty Rating

This will help you determine what kind of walk you are in for.

1. This is an easy, short walk with little to no rise in elevation. Good for young families.
2. This is a bit harder but still easy enough. There may be some elevation rise and rocks and roots on the trail. May be ½ mile or more to the tree and may include additional hiking if desired. Children will still enjoy this.

3. A good trip that may take some time to both get to the area of the tree and then find it. Some off-trail travel may be required. Could include wet areas to get through or some elevation gain up steep slopes. Older children with fair hiking skills and the proper equipment would enjoy the challenge.

4. An adventure for the experienced hiker, these will be off trail for the most part. Expect swamp tromping and bush-whacking. Will take considerable time to get to the tree and then find your way out. Plan ½ a day and go early so you are not trying to find your way out in the dark.

Keep in mind that the GPS coordinates have been supplied for the trees, but for some of the trips you will have to mark the coordinates for the access point so you can find your way back out of the woods. Take a compass reading also, who knows, you could lose your GPS power or signal and will have to depend on a map and compass.

Note on GPS coordinates

The format in this book is decimal-degrees. Be sure to go into your GPS settings and set it to that format. The old New Hampshire book was in degree-decimal-minute format. The new format is more commonly used.

Disclaimer

Please be aware of the weather and where you are going in the woods. It is up to you to have all the required equipment. Double-check the GPS readings for any long trips. We cannot be responsible for errors in this book. Trails and conditions can change, so please be aware that this book is but a guide. Respect the forest and enjoy these Big Trees.

About the Big Tree Program

The Big Tree Program is a national program that is run in each state to keep track of the largest trees in the states and the country. There are set guidelines on how to measure the trees, with trees re-measured every ten years in order to keep their champion status. In New Hampshire, there are over 1,100 trees that have been measured in the state list, with state and county champions shown. Under the best circumstances, each county has a team that measures any trees reported. The state coordinator will send out certificates to the owners and nominators and reports to the national group at American Forests. Vermont, Maine, and Massachusetts have smaller lists in their programs, mostly showing only the current state champs. Massachusetts also has a Legacy Tree listing showing historic and other important trees that have been measured. There are some National Champion trees in each state that are listed with American Forests.

How to Measure the Trees

After some time, you learn how to see the trees and where to look for them in the woods. Edges of clearings and along property boundaries or stonewalls are good places to start. I keep looking down low for large trunks or in the winter high up for wide crowns some distance off. They are harder to see in the summer, and you have to be closer because the trees around them have leafed out. Wandering is something I can do, and if you have heard of a tree in the area, sometimes it just takes that next hundred feet on the trail or around the next bend in the stream to find it.

Once you find a new tree it must be measured, so you need a tape to check the circumference around the trunk at 4½ feet up. If the ground at the trunk is sloped you measure from in between the high and low side or mid-slope at 4½ ft. That is your Circumference Breast Height or **CBH**. There are diameter tapes available that tell you the circumference and the diameter with one measurement. They are somewhat expensive, so a regular 25' tape will work if you do not plan to do much measuring. You can call in a measuring team at this point, and they can compare the tree to others on the list to see if it is close in size to other champions listed.

The measuring team will recheck the **CBH** and then measure the crown (how wide the branches spread out from the tree) with a 100-foot tape at the widest point and take another crown measurement at a right angle to that. The crown sizes are then added together and divided by 2 to get the Average Crown Spread or **ACS**.

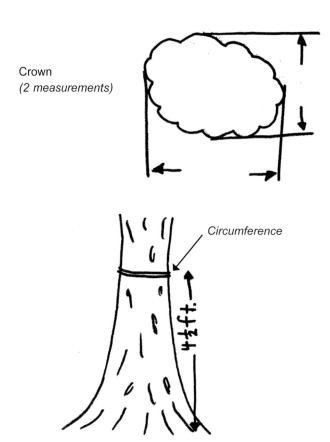

Crown
(2 measurements)

Circumference

4½ ft.

Then the height is checked with a clinometer, a calibrated instrument that is quite accurate if read right. Measure out from the tree 100 feet and then look through the clinometer, which gives a reading of the height from your eye up to the top of the tree. Then you sight the bottom of the tree and add or subtract this measurement from your tree height, depending on if you are higher or lower than the tree bottom at 100 feet away. What you end up with is your Vertical Height or **VH**. If you have been writing down these measurements, you will not have to recheck them as I often did. A GPS reading is then taken, and the tree is checked over to report the condition as excellent, good, fair, or poor.

For national champs and potential champs, more accurate measuring methods are now required, and the height is checked with a laser range-finder, which is better for leaning trees or wide-crowned trees where it is hard to pinpoint the highest branch on top. I used this tool for most of my height measurements. The spoke method is used for the crown spread, where you measure from the drip line of the branches to the trunk at several points around the tree, get an average, multiply by 2 (because you only

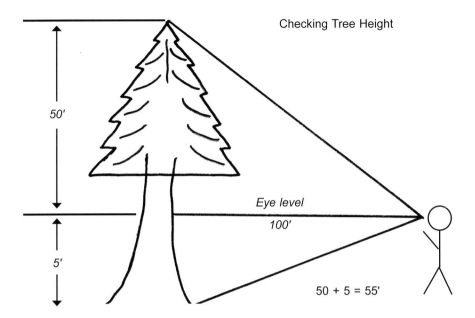

Checking Tree Height

50'

Eye level
100'

5'

50 + 5 = 55'

measured halfway), and then add the diameter of the trunk. Multi-trunk trees are also measured differently, with the trunks considered separate if the center pith line of each trunk meets below ground level. A national cadre of measurers have been trained (myself included) to more accurately measure these trees.

The tree is then scored in a point system and compared with others on the list. The total points are determined by adding the circumference in inches to the height in feet, then adding ¼ of the average crown spread. So, a tree with 75" CBH, 100' VH, and 60' ACS is scored as 75 + 100 + 15 = 190 total points.

Keep in mind that some types of trees just do not grow very large. You may not be very impressed by a champion gray birch or American chestnut unless you have some idea of what an average-sized tree of that species looks like. While you are out measuring, be sure to look at the other trees around, and if you come to a grove that consists of mostly one type of tree be sure to look for the largest one. Then, when you do see the champion of that type, you will appreciate it a bit more.

You can check your state's Big Tree website to compare sizes or for updates on some of the trees listed in this book.

- NH: http://extension.unh.edu/Trees/NH-Big-Tree-Program
- MA: Massachusetts Legacy Tree Program | Mass.gov
- VT: https://fpr.vermont.gov/forest/vermonts-forests/vermont-big-trees
- ME: Big Trees: Programs: Project Canopy: Help Trees help you. (maine.gov)

Maine

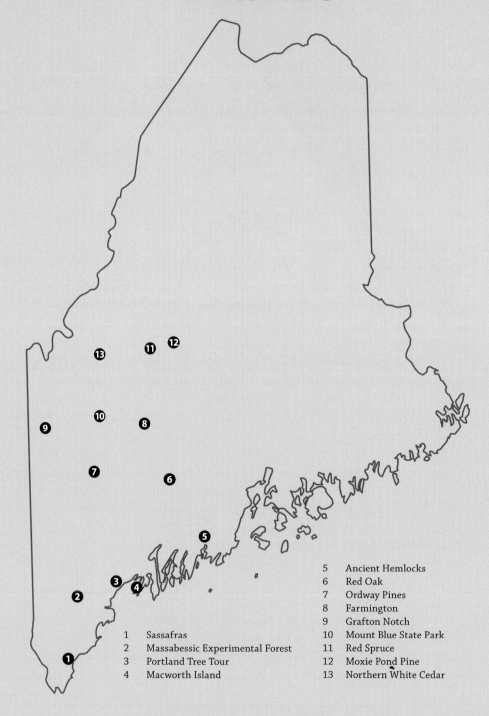

Sassafras *[Sassafras albidum (Nutt.) Nees]*

This walk in York will cover a lot of bases. It brings you to a cemetery, past several historic homes, into the woods, across a swinging bridge, along the harbor and to the beach, then into a few parks and through a small downtown area. You could even add an oceanside cliff walk if you have the time. Start out by parking in a small lot near the library. If you want to save the sassafras till the end, walk left when out of the parking area a short distance on Long Sands Road and follow Route 1A or York Street left again toward the ocean. One feature of this early settlement in Maine is the many interesting buildings you pass as you walk along the sidewalk to see the first few trees in Gilman Park. When arriving at the park, look on your right for some planted trees that have reached a pretty good size and are worth checking out. One is a tuliptree that has interesting shaped leaves, and, if seen in June, you likely will see its large tulip-like flowers. The dried-out petal remains are there all year long. This tree does not have the long, clear trunk many of this type have, as it branches out fairly low. There are also a few copper beeches here and an ash by the road. These all do not compete with the

Sassafras.

Wiggly Bridge. The world's smallest suspended bridge.

largest in the state but at some point, say fifty years from now, some will.

Continue on all the way to the ocean and take in the view at the beach and a small park bordering it. Go left along the waterfront to find the cliff walk if you decide to take the time. This is a beautiful walk along the ocean bringing you behind some homes along the edge of the rocky oceanfront. Be respectful of the property owners here, as there has been controversy over allowing access. Some of the homeowners want it to themselves, with townspeople insisting they have a right to walk here as they have for generations. I remember my Aunt Winnie bringing us here over fifty years ago and access was starting to be an issue then. Enjoy the walk and come back for lunch or a snack at the waterfront park. Be sure to search out an unusual sculpture on a rock here named "Pleasure Ground," with small statues depicting beachgoers in action.

After resting, head back on York Street a short distance and take one of the side roads on the left down to the river walk trail that brings you along the harbor front as the river goes inland. This is another beautiful area, with the working harbor-front shops, old homes, and boats at their moorings. The trail brings you to Route 103. Cross that and take the causeway to the "Wiggley Bridge" that was built in the 1930s and restored in 2016. It reminds one of the large steel suspension bridges on our roadways and as a pedestrian bridge gives us the perspective of one built to scale for walkers. On the other side of the bridge, the trail goes immediately into the woods and comes out in the housing area of York near the village.

The trails end at Mill Dam Road; follow that road to its end and go right a ½ mile along Lindsay Road, walking past some interesting homes up to the corner with York Street, where the cemetery on your right holds the most impressive sassafras trees in the state of Maine

Sassafras does not normally grow to a size to use for furniture in the north but does reach a size where it can be used to make canoe paddles. I have yet to try it, but some paddle makers will offer it as a specialized paddle wood, often at a higher cost. It can reach a larger size in some areas but is considered a pioneer species that grows quickly in clearings or after fires, then, as the other types of trees grow in and overshadow it, the sassafras will just as quickly die off. The orange wood is light and brittle but long-lasting in contact with the soil. It has been used for posts, barrels, and buckets, but most often the strong-smelling root bark is used to make a perfume. The root was also commonly boiled to make a tea, but large amounts have been found to cause cancer in lab tests, so that use is now banned. Some still consider it okay to use in small amounts, and I have tried the unique-flavored tea with no ill effects.

This small tree is found in many soil types and can grow by seed or root sprouts. You will find them in groups that spread quickly through an open area. One unique feature is that the leaves on a single tree can come in 3 different shapes: oval, three-lobed, and mitten-shaped. Keep in mind that not all trees will have the 3 shapes at any given time.

There are many large sassafras trees that you will see here. I would say this is the best site to view them in this size range in all of northern New England. The largest in the four states is here with others of comparable size. Be sure to take a look from the corner of Lindsay and Main Street, as the trees seen from that view look particularly good.

Difficulty Rating 2 Ocean edge on cliff walk.

Tuliptree

128" CBH   88' VH   58' ACS   Total Points 230   Poor Condition
GPS: N 43.13591°   W 070.64486°

Sassafras

84" CBH   66' VH   34' ACS   Total Points 158.5   Good Condition

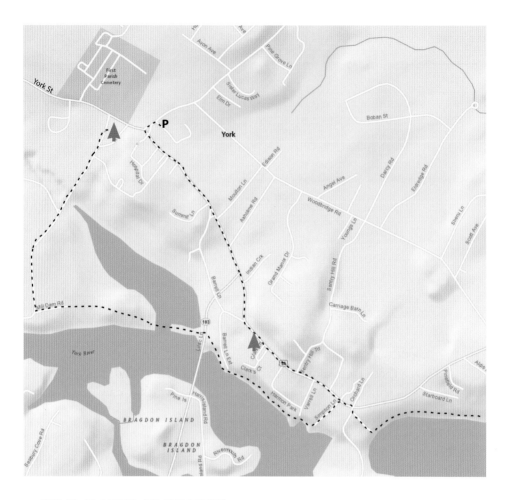

GPS: N 43.14375° W 070.65257°

Δ State Champion

Directions

From Route 1 go on Route 1A or York Street toward York Harbor about 1 mile to park at the library on the left.

Massabesic Experimental Forest

A lfred and Lyman, Maine, are home to this large state-run forestry experiment that had its origins from the great fire that swept the area in the 1940s. This is the same fire that went through the Ossipee area of New Hampshire, resulting in the pitch pine forests growing in afterwards there. In Maine, they took advantage of the catastrophic damage to the forest by starting a program of reseeding many white pines and growing some red pine in large areas along with experimenting on best forestry methods for the white pine.

Some of the trees that the fire missed on the SW part of the several thousand acre property have been noted as mature and old growth, so some of the section in Alfred was set aside as a preserve area by the state, and that is where this visit is located.

The BC Jordan and Littlefield trails bring you through the woods and showcase these trees along with other features of the landscape.

While this is one of several Maine properties that have trees not

Moss at cedar swamp.

Shawn Martin and Atlantic white cedar.

yet in the Big Tree category, it is on the very edge, with many in the 9–10-foot-circumference range. The future looks very good for its Big Tree capacity, as the quantity and quality of mature trees is great. Because there are so many and they support one another, few will be lost to the wind, barring a major hurricane coming inland.

I was particularly impressed by a hemlock on the Littlefield Trail that is among the best in Maine. Its circumference is a little lacking, but it makes up for that with its height of 110 feet. That is a feature of many trees in this area, with heights of up to 120 feet on the few that I checked.

The other important feature of these woods is the Atlantic white cedar swamps, the most extensive in Maine. Because it is at the north-ern-most end of their range, the trees are smaller than those found along the southern Atlantic coast, but the Maine state champ for that species is located here. You can see an example that is almost the same size as the champion by following the Clayton Carl Trail to Cedar Overlook and going down into the outskirts of the swamp. The champion itself is on the other side, near the center of the swamp, and the terrain is somewhat sensitive. Too many people traipsing around could be an issue, so I hope you are happy seeing this tree, which is a little smaller but has that nice, clear wood going up the trunk for about ten feet that makes it a great example. Comparing it to others nearby, you will get an idea of how hard it is to get clear lumber from cedar.

You can also access this tree from the other side of the property by walking on Government Road to see how the property is being managed. There are many large pines scattered along the road and in the woods with younger trees growing up around them. This requires a bushwhack from the road to the cedars, so map and compass or GPS should be used to be sure you can get back to the road again in a timely manner.

There are many plantings of trees such as red pine and scotch pine, so it would be a good idea to look at the website for the property and also to visit the Alfred Conservation Commission website for maps and descriptions of the trails.

Difficulty Rating 2

Trail Cedar

63" CBH   56' VH   19' ACS   Total Points 124   Good Condition
GPS: N 43.443935°   W 070.667833°

Champion Cedar

70" CBH   60' VH   19' ACS   Total Points 136   Good Condition
No GPS
Δ State Co-Champion

Directions

From Route 111 in Alfred, take Kennebunk Road toward Kennebunk. Go just under 1 mile and bear right at a fork on Mouse Lane. Go just under a mile again, and, if going to see the mature trees on the BC Jordan and Littlefield trails, go straight on Ida Jim Road to the gate at the end and walk down the road to the trail on the right. The Clayton Carleton Trail to the cedars is on the left.

If going to the cedars from the other side of the property, bear right

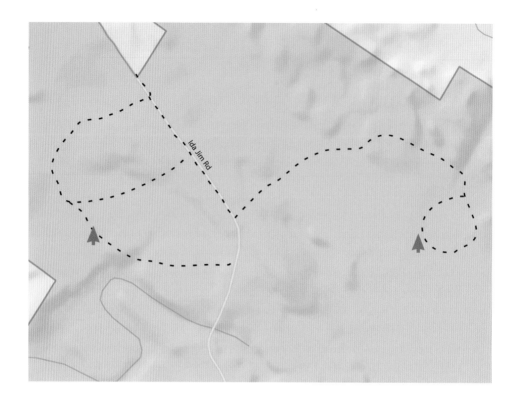

to stay on Mouse Lane and go 1.7 miles to its end and turn left onto Whichers Mill Road, and go 1.2 miles to a gate on Government Road. Walk on Government Road for 1 mile, then bushwhack about 1,000 feet into the woods on the left to the cedar swamp. The tree is on the edge of the swamp.

Portland Tree Tour

This largest city in Maine has a few outstanding spots where you can see some large oaks. Highlights include Baxter Woods and Deering Oaks Park, along with some hemlocks in the Evergreen Cemetery. This seaport is quite large and busy, so there is much to do and see. South Portland has several prominent points with old forts and lighthouses on the waterfront. A bike or walking trail takes you along the shore from Bug Light along the South Portland Greenbelt across the Casco Bay Bridge to the Eastern Promenade Trail to Fish Point with Fort Allen Park. The docks in Portland have cruise boats full of tourists arriving in the summer and fall. Local ferry boats are also available to take you out to nearby islands and other more distant destinations. Restaurants line the docks along with many nearby shops. The city is part working waterfront and part tourist destination. Biking along the trails is good but to visit some of the trees on bikes you have to cross some of the busy highway off- and on-ramps, which can be dangerous. I would suggest riding your bike to the trees in the northern section and then walk or use caution if biking around Deering Oaks Park. The park

Siberian elm at Deering Oaks Park.

Deering oak and Shawn Martin.

is impressive, with many good-sized oaks, some Austrian pine, and the state champion Siberian elm and green ash. A pond in the center has a mini-house on a small island that will attract your attention. Seagulls seem to love it here and flock all around. The best white oak to see is in this part of the park not far from the pond. A busy main road separates the two sections of the park.

Deering Oaks was first set aside in 1879, and forestry groups have been planting trees ever since. Some large trees were lost in recent storms, but new replacements have been planted, with care taken to be sure they will impress as they grow to great size. In the part of the park between State and High streets, you will find three state champion trees. The green ash near State Street is the largest in northern New England and quite impressive, especially with the leaves off and its intricate, small branching silhouetted against a cloudy sky. It is quite prevalent in the Midwest and South but not so common around here. Its use as lumber is said to be similar to white ash but not considered to be quite as good. The Siberian elm is next if you head toward the Rose

Circle in the center of this part of the park. Brittle in nature, it is thought of as invasive because it is not natural to the area and can spread quite readily. This one is good-looking, with fissured bark and its attractive flow of leaves and branches. The pin oak is on the other side of the Rose Circle near High Street. This is said to have the largest crown spread of any tree in Maine, at 106 feet. Also called swamp oak, it is native to the wet areas in the middle part of the country, but is frequently planted in parks and cemeteries in New England.

Make your way to Baxter Woods by car or bike and park on the side of Stevens Road at the trailhead. You will notice a group of red pines planted nearby as you head down the trail. There are several good-sized trees in the woods, with oaks, red pines, and basswoods that will draw your gaze. These woods, once owned by the former mayor, James Phinney Baxter, were set aside in his honor by his son Percival to be "forever kept in its wild state as a sanctuary for wild birds." He also donated the land at Baxter State Park that includes Mount Katahdin in northern Maine. Be sure to make the loop around and stop at the oak with an unusual trunk on your way back toward the trailhead.

The Evergreen Cemetery should be your next stop, just a quarter mile across the road. Entering at the main entrance, you will shortly see the state champion Austrian pine. It's an unusual-looking tree with many branches curling up from the trunk. The current measurement was

Oddly shaped Austrian pine.

Aura around this green ash.

from the only place it could be measured as a single trunk while omitting another separate trunk. At some point, it likely will be re-measured by measuring the multiple trunks added together in a formula that would give what is called a functional circumference. A special tree at any rate.

It won't take long for you to notice the many buildings and monuments along with many graves of past important citizens from Portland. Take some time to look around and work your way to the back part within sight of the ponds. Here you can wander over to the edge of the hill to a grove of hemlocks that are of grand size. They do not have that old-growth look and likely grew pretty fast in this open setting. Some have lost their tops and none are very tall, but one big one is doing well, and at almost 155" in circumference is about the biggest around you will see in Maine.

Difficulty rating 2   Distance and traffic.

1. White Oak Deering Park

160" C   76' VH   48' ACS   Total Points 248   Good Condition
GPS: N 43.65956°   W 070.27124°

2. Green Ash

131" CBH   86' VH   59' ACS   Total Points 232   Excellent Condition
GPS: N 43.659319°   W 070.269040°
Δ State Champion

3. Siberian Elm

170" CBH   61' VH   88' ACS   Total Points 280   Good Condition
GPS: N 43.659093°   W 070.268456°
Δ State Champion

4. Pin Oak

163" CBH   89' VH   106' ACS   Total Points 279, 2015 measurements   Fair Condition
GPS: N 43.658786°   W 070.267967°
Δ State Champion

5. Red Pine Baxter Woods

GPS: N 43.67707°   W 070.28903°

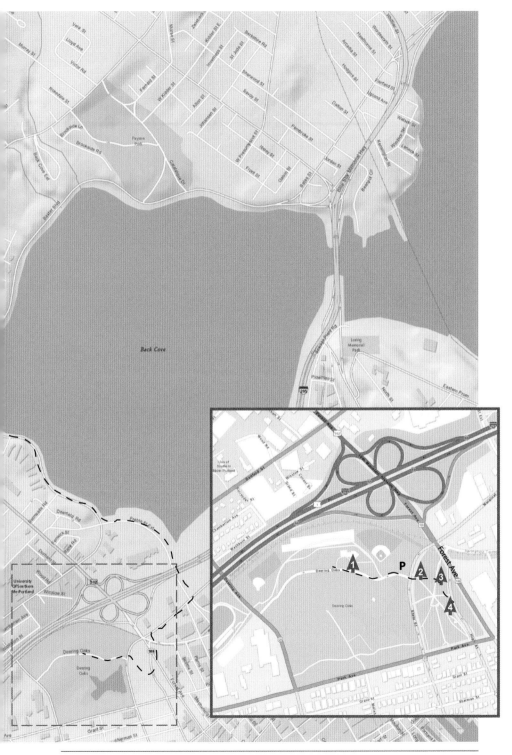

Large circumference hemlock at Evergreen Cemetery.

6. Oak Baxter Woods

GPS: N 43.67613° W 070.29266°

7. Austrian Pine, evergreen

176" CBH   67' VH   55' ACS   Total Points 256   Good Condition
GPS: N 43.681134° W 070.295231°
Δ State Champion

8. Hemlock

154" CBH   78' VH   68' ACS   Total Points 249   Good Condition
GPS: N 43.68315° W 070.30237°

Directions

Get off I-295 in Portland on Forest Avenue heading south. Take the 1st right and you are at Deering Oaks and can start looking for a parking spot. You could also take I-295 to Franklin Street and go 0.6 mi. to the waterfront area then take a left onto Fore Street and go about a ½ mile to park at the Eastern Promenade and bike from there.

Macworth Island

Plan a visit to this former home site of Percival Baxter for a coastal walk with ocean views on a trail through the variety of large trees that were intentionally planted there. Baxter was governor of Maine from 1921 to 1924. The island was first inhabited by a Native American Wabanaki tribal leader. Arthur Macworth was the first colonial settler who lived here, starting in 1634 and giving the island its name. In

Maine Big Tree coordinator Jan Santerre and Austrian pine.

Old stone dock.

1946, Governor Baxter donated the property to the state along with the land he owned up north that is now Baxter State Park. The Baxter mansion was later donated along with funding to create the Baxter School for the Deaf that is now in the center of the one-hundred-acre island.

Andrew Avenue takes you out to the island across a long narrow causeway up to a gate house at the entrance for the school. You can park in a parking area on the right after the gate. A fee is charged here. There is only room for twenty cars, and there is no other parking, so you may want to plan an off-hour or off-season visit. Start off along the trail and see a few medium sized American elms that are in good condition. I was told the ocean winds may have kept the elm disease at bay by blowing the evil spores back toward the mainland and keeping these isolated island trees safe. You will soon come to the largest diameter Scotch or "Scots" pine that I have seen. It is somewhat short though at 57'. Those ocean winds may have taken some top branches off. These pines are easy to recognize by the beige color of the top third of the tree.

Scots pines have been planted all throughout New England, and you can see them along roadsides and in public parks and cemeteries. Continue along to the next tree, a black or Austrian pine that is a standout for northern New England. It is also in the fifty-foot range for height but has a large diameter compared to other black pines that I have seen. I have never had the chance to use either of these woods in my work but understand that Scots pine is used for furniture and many of the same uses as our white pine. In fact, it was a source of ships masts in the UK, where it is native, until they used it up and came for our pines. Austrian pine is said to be used for pulpwood, crates, and construction lumber.

Continue on the trail around the island and look for the many types of trees planted all around. Norway spruce abound with fairy houses built at their bases. Red pine are scattered in a few spots, with many natural-grown hardwoods growing in. Be sure to check out the pet cemetery at the eastern section of the island where several of Baxter's Irish setters and other pets were put to rest. He must surely have appreciated his pets, giving them this wonderful site near the Atlantic Ocean with perpetual care for the cemetery funded by an endowment in his will.

Get back on the loop trail and enjoy the rest of the walk. Some carvings of faces were added over time. Keep an eye out for the Listening Tree about ¾ of the way around the island. The hollow trunk has a growth inside that looks like a human ear, which made this a special tree to the students of the Baxter School. The state champ shagbark hickory was also on the island at one time but was lost in a storm that took many trees in the area, requiring a major cleanup by the forestry professionals out of Portland who are in charge of this gem of a spot.

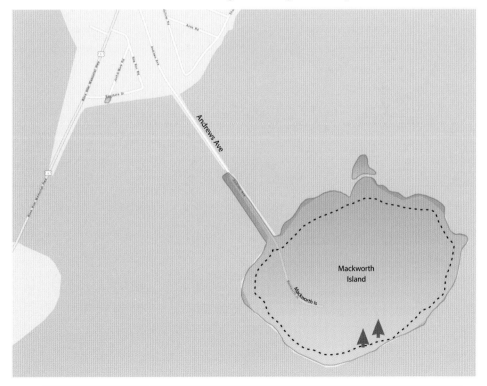

Scots Pine

129" CBH   57' VH   46' ACS   Total Points197   Good Condition
GPS: N 43.68685°   W 070.23116°
Δ State Champion

Austrian Pine

106" CBH   57' VH   49' ACS   Total Points 175   Fair Condition
GPS: N 43.68700°   W 070.23050°

Directions

Take I-295 N heading east out of Portland and get on Route 1 N. Go over the bridge and a little over a mile to Andrews Avenue on the right. Follow that over the causeway to the island.

Ancient Hemlocks *[Tsuga canadensis]*

I deal for a quick stop off Route 1, these hemlocks appear as soon as you leave the parking area. The loop trail brings you through the hemlocks and after a good twenty-minute walk around the trail, back into the hemlocks again. Some of these trees were measured and cored for age back in the 1980s and described then as one of the few upland hemlock forests in Maine that are not associated with white pines on sandy soil near wetlands, or not on steep ravines and riverbanks. This forest is on rich soil in a poorly drained flat site, making it unusual in the state of Maine. At that time, one was measured at 40" diameter with a few others close to that size recorded. The ages were from 170 to 240

Brian Martin and Abby with biggest hemlock.

years, so now would be 210 to 280 years old. The woods are dark in the area of the roughly six acres of older growth where the craggy-barked old trees dominate the landscape. The undergrowth includes quite a bit of Indian cucumber and trillium near the trail as you first get going. You will also see striped maple spread around, and, although I did not look for it, they recorded a large one at 7" diameter in the study that may have grown to champion status by now. We walked through looking for the largest hemlock they had measured many years ago, and, although there are several good-sized ones with that old look, the trees kept coming up with smaller measurements than the biggest in the study. After taking the loop and coming back thinking it was no longer there, we came to a junction and a real big one was off to the side there. It measured 45" diameter compared to the 40" D or 125" CBH 1980 measurement. I thought that to be pretty slow-growing until I checked the big fallen hemlock trunk behind it. The wind had blown this hollow tree over years ago, but there was still enough trunk standing to measure and I got 151" CBH or 48" diameter and thought this is likely the largest measured back then. I was still impressed by the standing tree though, making a statement in this old looking forest in coastal Maine.

The town of Waldoboro, which owns the property, has recently improved the trails and is making efforts to prevent the spread of woolly adelgid that was found on some trees. They are actively working with the Maine State Forest Service and released a type of beetle that preys on the adelgids with the idea that over time the beetles should control the infestation. Seeing the devastating results from the adelgid in Massachusetts, I sincerely hope they stem the tide.

This is a great stop off busy Route 1 where you can get the feel of an ancient forest in a short amount of time.

Difficulty Rating 1 May be wet in some areas.

142" CBH 80' VH 49' ACS Total Points 234 Good Condition
GPS: N 44.097248° W 69.408463°

Directions

Coming from the south on Route 1, look for the Park and Ride on the right at the junction of West Main Street. Pull in the parking area and find a place to park. It might be full on some weekdays. A sign for "Ancient Hemlocks" is at the back, and the trail starts toward the south end of the parking area.

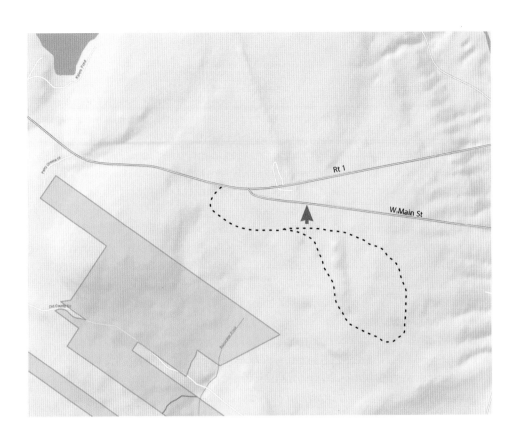

Red Oak *[Quercus rubra]*

Riverside in Augusta is the place to go in Maine if you want to see the state's largest red oak. It is in a wooded area next to the Kennebec River off the Augusta Greenway Trail, with a side path through the woods that brings you right to the tree. The fun way to see it is to bring your bike and start from one of the Kennebec Rail Trail parking areas. Pedal along the river behind the downtown stores and restaurants, then cross the bridge to Old Fort Western. Follow the Greenway Trail past a playground park, a boat landing, under the bridge, to several historic sites, the arsenal, and then the huge oak in the quiet woods.

If you want to get your history fix, then stop at the Old Fort Western as part of your visit here. Known as the oldest wooden fort in the country, it was used by Benedict Arnold when he attacked Quebec during the American Revolution. Originally built in 1754 by a Boston merchant, who with support from French Canadians, wanted to take control of lands used by the native Abenaki tribes.

Fort Western in Augusta.

Huge red oak.

After checking out the fort, walk or ride along the trail that heads out behind some buildings and parking lots until you come to the armory with its impressive stone buildings and granite boat landing. This property was sold by the city to a developer who has plans to save the buildings by restoring them to their former glory and adding retail or residential tenants. Until that time, it is off limits to public use, so stay on the trail as you go by. At the end of the open area just past a cable gate, look for a small trail on the left that takes you up into the woods a short distance to the big red oak.

This is another example of how large some of our hardwoods can get on the banks of the big rivers in the northeast. This site on the Kennebec provides plenty of sunlight and water to feed this behemoth and keep it growing until old age takes its toll. At 240" in circumference, this is a size range that few hardwoods in NE can reach. I assume it grew in the open here for some period then the other trees were allowed to grow in around it.

Red oak has been a staple for lumber in the area and at times can warrant a good price at the lumber retail stores. It is a common tree in northern New England, producing high-quality wood for furniture and veneer. In my work, I have used the wood for lapstrake canoe keels, stems, and gunwales, as well as for furniture and the beams for my new boat shed. It is an important firewood source, being readily available and producing heat through the night. The acorns are a staple for wildlife, with deer, bear, squirrels, chipmunks, turkeys, and blue jays depending on them to get through the winter. During my visit, the shadow of an eagle kept flashing through the woods as it circled up above in the sunlight.

After visiting this tree, you can work your way to your vehicle or continue on your bike up Arsenal Road to the end and right across the street you will see the entrance to the Viles Arboretum. This was started in the 1980s, so the trees are not large but you can brush up on your ID skills by checking the different groves planted here. I was particularly impressed with the larch grove that has a small lane separating it from a green ash planting on the opposite side.

Another place to visit is Vaughan Woods in nearby Gardner. You could even start or end your bike ride near there. These woods have some old and tall pine and hemlock growing near the banks of a stream with trails and stone-arch bridges on both sides. The original owners of the estate have reported that some of the trees here at one time were marked with the King's Broad Arrow, claiming them as mast trees for the Royal Navy. They also supplied some trees for use in the USS *Constitution* in the US Navy.

Although the trees there now are not real big in diameter, they are among the tallest in Maine, measuring to 130' tall.

Difficulty Rating 1–2   if biking to Vaughan Woods.

240" CBH   67' VH   89' ACS   Total Points 329   Fair Condition
GPS: N 44.30568°   W 069.77063°
Δ Former State Champion

Directions

From the center of Augusta, get on Water Street heading north. Go right on Bridge Street/Route 27 and over the bridge spanning the Kennebunk River. Take a right into the parking lot for the Augusta Parks Dept. Walk over toward the Old Fort Western and the trail near the river. It's about a ½ mile to the tree. If biking, you can start at the Downtown Parking area off Water Street as shown on the map or at Granite City Park next to the river off Route 201 in Hallowell and ride 3 miles along the rail trail to the greenway and the tree.

Ordway Pines

This journey to see some nice old-growth pines and hemlocks brings you to the small town of Norway, Maine, and a town forest on Lake Pennesseewassee. Samuel Ames was the first settler in Norway, arriving in 1759 to build a house and small mill. He owned and cared for the woods on his land, known then as Ames Woods, until he passed away in 1852.

A few years later, they were sold to John Ordway; he changed the name of the woods to Ordway Grove. Later, the land changed hands several times, with logging of the woods proposed by some, but the trees ended up being conserved by a group called the Twin Town Nature Club and became a public park in 1931. Look for these towering trees rising over the town while driving in on Main Street.

The trail to see the pines starts off Pleasant Street, on the left where you will see a sign directing walkers down the trail next to a garage and on past a kiosk into the property. It will not be long until the Big Trees start showing up, and you will be impressed. There are many old trees here and they are very tall. Some could be the tallest in Maine, with recorded measurements of over 150'.

The pine with the biggest circumference, at 147", is right next to the trail and easy to find. The old-growth characteristics show up with the deeply fissured bark that has been broken into horizontal chunks by the frost over the long winters. If you look around from here and further

Pines as seen from downtown Norway.

Former County Forester Merle Ring (right) and Michele Windsor (left).

along the trail, you will notice the many old-growth trees around. In other woods, some old growth, such as hemlocks, will not get as large, but will have the same impressive bark characteristics. If you walk further along the trail, you will come across a hemlock that has a decent height. Keep on going to see the lake and really appreciate what this area has to offer with the waterfront trail and this grove of magnificent pines within walking distance of the downtown area.

Difficulty Rating 1

White Pine

147" CBH   133' VH   50' ACS   Total Points 292   Good Condition
GPS: N 44.215407°   W 70.548924°

Hemlock

116" CBH   112.5' VH   49' ACS   Total Points 240   Excellent Condition
GPS: N 44.2215290°   W 70.549300°

Directions

From Route 26 in Norway get on Main Street or Route 118 heading west. Take a right on Pleasant Street just before the lake, and 5 or 6 houses down, near a white house and garage, there is a sign on the left for the trail. You can park on the side of the road or park in town and walk about a ½ mile to the trail.

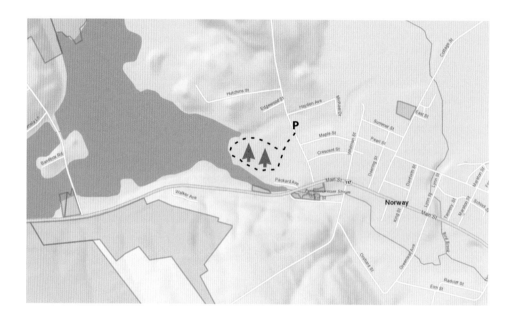

Farmington Village Tour

This busy small city is the home of the University of Maine Farmington, with a campus near the center of town. The school, several parks, fairgrounds, and the storefronts are all in close proximity along with a few Big Trees right in the heart of town that the locals seem quite proud of. The town has made an effort to promote walking tours of historic sites with Walk Around Farmington signs highlighting these special places. That, along with the Big Trees, allows for a good walk showcasing the best in town, with spots for breaks and shopping while you're at it. The library is a particularly impressive building, so be sure to check it out.

Signs will show you where public parking is located off Maine Street, and you can park and make your way to the Meetinghouse Park to start your tour.

The green space for the park was set aside in 1802 and eventually used to hold livestock while the farmers came to the meetinghouse that was across the street. The meetinghouse burned down in the late 1800s and the park was eventually improved with a Civil War monument and other historic markers that were put in place. Now it is in its glory with an added gazebo where many events draw the townsfolk to this central

Meetinghouse Park in Farmington.

Octagon House and tuliptree.

location. It's an ideal place to start since and you will also notice a pretty nice oak to get you going with appreciating the trees.

Walk across Main Street and a short distance down Anson Street beside the courthouse to the last of three large white pines that were once in town. The other two had to be cut or had died since I started the book. This survivor is picture-perfect as a downtown tree tucked in next to Central Cemetery and the courthouse. Go back to Main Street and follow along till you get to Broadway Street and go down until you get to the junction of High Street. Look across the street you can see the tuliptree on the corner. This is on the grounds of the Octagon House, which is now owned by the historical society in town. The tuliptree is said to be about one hundred years old and is rare to find this far north.

For trees in a more wooded setting, you follow High Street past the North Church, take a right on Court Street, and follow it all the way till you get to North Street, go left, walk up the hill, and start looking for a trail into Bonney Woods on your left. You could drive to a parking

Bonney Woods hemlock.

area on Anson Street if you're in a rush or not up for the walk. This small woodlot has many old hemlocks, some of which have reached Big Tree status. To find the biggest, work your way through the lot to the main entrance on Anson Street. There is a sign for Bonney Woods and the hemlock is near the sign. At 138" in circumference, it is among the largest in girth in Maine, but the height is only 83' so it loses out there. What may have been the largest tree in this lot was laying in the woods near this road with a hollow center. It was cut up after it fell, but you may still see it there. Further still, there is a small cemetery on the top of a hill that would top off your visit to these dark woods. Anson Street is quite busy, with no sidewalk on the upper part, so you may want to go back to town the way you came. Be sure to visit some of the shops, grab a bite to eat, and see some more of the interesting places in this quintessential western Maine town.

Difficulty Rating 2

Octagon House Tuliptree

151" C   89' VH   54' ACS   Total Points 253   Fair Condition
GPS: N 44.671276°   W 70.149356°

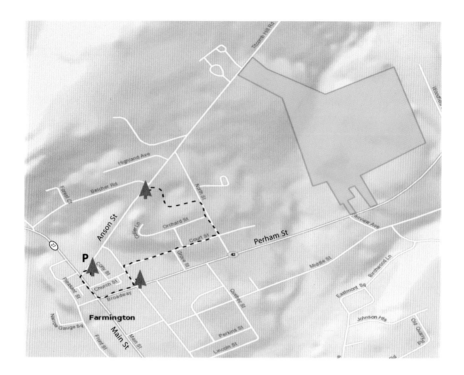

Courthouse Pine

144" CBH   89' VH   60' ACS   Total Points 248   Good Condition
GPS: N 44.67174° W 70.15192°

Hemlock

138" CBH   83' VH   42' ACS   Total Points 232   Good Condition
GPS: N 44.67528° W 70.14881°

Directions

Take Route 2 until it meets Route 27 or Main Street, in Farmington.

Grafton Notch

I saw mention of old growth in Grafton Notch and was not expecting much for Big Trees. Many old-growth woods do not reach great size, and with the higher mountain setting, I was expected smaller trees. What a surprise with the great old yellow birch along the Table Rock Trail. While these are not the largest in the state of Maine, they are well worth the visit, and if you have never been through the notch, you are in for a treat. My trip in late October, in peak foliage season, encountered surprisingly little traffic the afternoon we went, with only two other cars in the parking lot. I'm sure it would be a different story on a holiday weekend earlier in the year. On the way through the notch, other places to stop and check out include Screw Auger Falls, the Moose Cave, and Mother Walker Falls.

To see the trees, pull into the parking area for the hiking trails where the AT crosses the road. In season, you will have to pay the fee of $3 for Maine residents, $4 for nonresidents. The kiosk shows a loop trail on the other side of the road that goes up the AT, over to Table Rock, and back down the red trail. This side of the road has a loop trail up to the "eyebrow" and back or a hike up to Old Speck. There are more old-growth trees just north of Mahoosuc Notch on this side, but that is a longer and tougher hike so I did not check them out. Keep in mind that the

Grafton Notch from Table Rock.

Guarding the trail.

Mahoosuc section of the AT is considered the most difficult in the whole length from Georgia to Maine, so do not take any hike here lightly. Even the somewhat short 2.3-mile hike to Table Rock has difficult rocks to go over and steep sections that take sure footing to go down. If you are not up to the hike, you can still see the trees by going up the Red Trail at the AT trail junction, with the Big Trees all before the steep parts, and then turn around to make a short jaunt out of it. Otherwise, take the AT trail to the junction of the Red Trail and check out the 125" CBH gnarly, old mountain sentry of a yellow birch standing guard and telling you that you should take care if going this way. Those that want a serious climb can go up this way. If not, take the AT up to the blue trail to Table Rock and back down the same way for a safer trip, or make it a round trip by way of the steeper Red Trail down.

On the way, keep an eye out for more yellow birch. All stages of growth can be seen here, showing how the bark changes depending on the age and growing conditions. After what seems like quite a stretch of gradual uphill hiking, you will come to a nice spot near a stream where there is a sign at the junction with the Blue Trail. Keep going up the still steeper Blue Trail past a medium-sized, smooth barked yellow birch and on to a jumble of rocks signifying that you are getting close to the top.

Follow the red markers.

When you come to a ledge with built-in steel ladder rungs, you are at last at Table Rock. Scramble up the rungs to an impressive view looking over the notch and across to Old Speck.

When rested, tear yourself away from the view and find the Red Trail going down on the right before getting back to the ladder rungs. This trail brings you around and under the Table Rock ledges while working its way down the steep slope. Rock jumbles, caves, very large boulders, and a sign saying "drop off" can be expected.

You should spend some time making your way down around all this, and, when near the bottom, start looking for large yellow birch and a few maples. These beauties will make the hike feel worthwhile as your special reward after all the hard work. I did not measure any other trees here as it was getting dark, so you may want to check a few out and see if there is one larger than the sentry tree at the junction. At the AT, go left and back to the road and your vehicle. If it's near lunch or dinnertime, you may want to picnic at the Spruce Meadow Picnic Area, with wildlife viewing and Old Speck to keep you happy. Wildlife that could be asso- ciated with this hike are the peregrine falcons that nest along the high ledges and that birdwatchers come flocking to see.

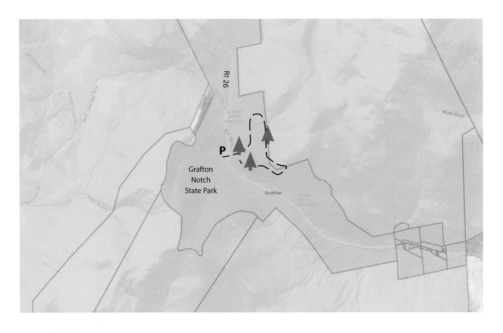

Difficulty Rating 3   Steep areas

Yellow Birch Sentry

125" CBH   60' VH   47' ACS   Total Points 197   Fair Condition
GPS: N 44.59097° W 70.94491°

Smooth Barked Birch

80" CBH   82' VH
GPS: N 44.58994° W 70. 93575°   ¾ of the way up to table rock.

Big Surprise—Needs Measuring

GPS: N 44.58870° W 70.94308°

Directions

From Bethel, take Route 2 N about 5 ½ miles and go left in Newry on
Route 26. Travel about 12 miles to the AT parking on the left.

Mount Blue State Park

T he state champion red pine can be seen in Mount Blue State Park, not far from Farmington. The park is in two sections, with the Mount Blue and Center Hill in one, and then a beach and campground on Webb Lake. Mount Blue offers an incredible backdrop rising from the opposite shore of the lake when looking from the beach area where the tree is located. In season, you drive to the campground and the lake by following the signs on Route 142 to Webb Beach Road and the campground entrance. A fee is paid at the booth and you continue toward the beach on the left. In the winter, Webb Beach Road is plowed just enough to allow parking for a few cars, and you have to park there and snowshoe or ski along the snowmobile trail on the road to the campground entrance. A winter trip would be about three miles in and out while, if in season, the trip is about one mile. Once on the road to the beach, keep a look out for the turn to the nature center and park there for a walk past an amphitheater and to the lake and the beach. The view is amazing, and the trees here are mostly your northern species with red spruce all over, white cedar, white pine here and there, with birch, maple, and poplars mixed in. Cross by the swimming beach to a picnic area spread throughout the woods with tables and grills set up to use.

Mount Blue.

Red pine.

Along the trail, the one red pine stands out with its tall reddish trunk and thin flaking bark. This tree's home range is in the northern part of New England, and as you go south the pitch pine tends to take over for it. Look for the tell-tale 2"-long cones and the clusters of two needles, while the pitch pines have three needles and prickly cones. This pine looks to be healthy, but in southern New Hampshire, many of the planted red pine are being attacked by insects and a control method of cutting infected areas down seems to be the only way to fight it. I have hopes that it will be some time before the insects make it up to this part of Maine. Be sure to hang out a while under the pine and spruce to enjoy a snack while taking in the tree and the area.

To see a few other Big Trees while here, follow the trail along the shore toward the South Shelter. One nice white pine stands out with its massive roots showing next to the trail. It's big enough to be noteworthy in Maine, and the setting next to the lake is outstanding. If you want, continue on a bit further to see the shelter set in a wooded cove. What a nice spot to reserve for an outing base where you could then explore the park with a group.

Head back the way you came and then out toward the road. Just as you are leaving the parking area, keep an eye out to the left. There is a big pine just in the woods there that measures out at 147" circumference and has a good height of 128'. This is comparable to the Ordway Pines in Norway. You will not see too many of this size in Maine, so take a good look. There could be more that I did not find in this park, so with a little searching you might find others here that are of significance in the state.

Difficulty rating 1

Red Pine

93" CBH   90' VH   36' ACS   Total Points 192   Excellent Condition
GPS: N 44.67671° W 070.44032°
Δ Listed as State Co-champion

Lakeshore Pine

140" CBH   93' VH   47' ACS   Total Points 245   Good Condition
GPS: N 44.67557° W 070.43817°

Biggest Pine

147" CBH   128' VH   48' ACS   Total Points 287   Good Condition
GPS: N 44.67727° W 070.44366°

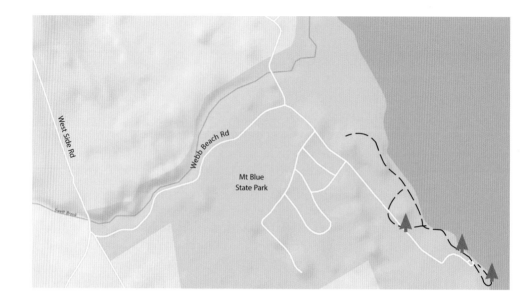

Directions

Take 142 South out of the center of Weld about 6 miles and take a right onto West Side Road. Go 3.5 miles and take a right onto Webb Beach Road, then go into the state park. Note the $5 resident $7 non resident fees.

Red Spruce *[Picea rubens]*

T his is a great hike to see old-growth red spruce in a setting that shows off how it grows in deep, dark forests on the steep, northern slopes of the mountains. This species is tenacious in its ability to sprout up and hang on along the cold, rocky ledges. They are growing their best along the mid-elevations of around 2400' in Maine. You can see small spruce about a foot tall that are twenty to thirty years old mixed in with medium-sized forty-footers and a slow-growing, large specimen with a 96" CBH and 81' VH that is likely over two-hundred years old. These moss-covered woods have areas that show how blow-downs open up space for the young sprouts to get started. In other areas, they are a little older and so thick you can hardly walk through, then you break into some roomier spots where the bigger trees are located.

Much of the spruce at lower elevations has been cut over throughout this paper company land that has been logged for generations and is now

Pretty rough trail.

second- or third-growth forests. The spruce that grew up higher on steep ledges was hard to get to, so some was not cut, leaving behind what is called old growth. The age of these old forests can vary depending on whether there was a wind or fire disturbance on the different mountaintops before any logging took place.

The hike is a moderate climb in the AT corridor along a narrow trail covered with rocks and roots, making it tough going at times. Start at a parking area near Pleasant Pond with a sign telling the distances up and beyond. If you park at the second parking area further along East Road, it will save you some hiking time. Start off and go past a sign for a lean-to that through-hikers use and get going up the mountain. I noticed some fair-sized poplar (big tooth aspen) on the way. About a third of the way up, you will come to the big spruce on the left. It is just off the trail and the trunk is hidden by smaller trees; you could pass it by unless you keep a constant watch, so you may want to use your GPS. This is not the biggest red spruce in the state but is in a size range that is very large for this species. We had gone up the mountain and to the slopes of nearby Middle Mountain to search for some other trees that were found in the 1990s and recorded in the 30" diameter range then, but we could not locate them. The hike up and off trail searching through dense underbrush wore me out, so we were okay with the tree we found on the way up. If anyone wants to look around the northeast sides of the Pleasant Pond mountains, you may find several that were reported in that range. Just be sure to study a map of the area, then

Spruce and fall colors and Mosquito Mt.

bring it and a compass, and use them, along with plotting the AT location on your GPS, so you can find your way back. Maybe you will find a taller tree that could be the new state champ.

There was some coyote scat on the top of the mountain, so I can associate this tree with them. The American marten starts its geological range here, and this is the type of dense forest cover they would thrive in. My experience with the spruce found in most building-supply stores is that it is not resistant to decay. The old leather-bound Audel Carpentry books printed in 1923 contradicts this, and describes the wood as resistant to decay and used for submerged cribs and cofferdams. Some woods do better when constantly under water, and that may be the case here.

Difficulty Rating 3–4 Steep trail; use caution if searching with GPS for other trees.

96" CBH   81' VH   34' ACS   Total Points 186   Fair to Good Condition
GPS: N 45.26304°   W 069.88984°

Directions

From 201 in Caratunk, take a right on School Street or Main Street to the center of town and take Pleasant Pond Road. Go about 4.5 miles and past Pleasant Mountain Pond to a right on North Cove Road to the end, then go left a short distance to parking on the left. Connect over to the AT.

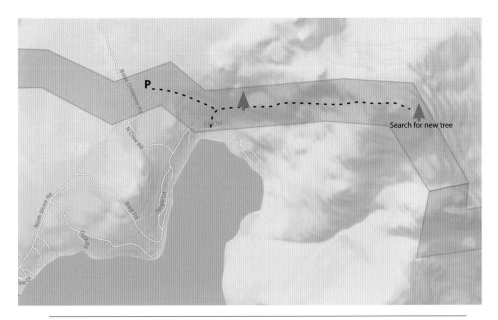

Moxie Pond Pine

A pine along the shore of a lake is always nice to see, and this one shows up by rising above the other trees if seen while driving along the shore of Moxie Pond. With the sun from the lake on one side and a clearing for power lines on the other, considering that it is in good condition and has a steady supply of water, this pine should keep gaining in size. Outside of the camps along the lakeshore, the land is mostly Weyerhaeuser lumber company land. They recently purchased Plum Creek Timber Co., which owned the 860,000 acres with large holdings in the upper Kennebec River area, around Moosehead Lake, and bordering Flagstaff Lake. While driving in and out along the roads, be aware that they are used by logging trucks that you must give way to because they cannot stop easily. So be careful when rounding corners— be sure the way is clear. Also keep in mind that there are several bridge

Maine state forester Patty Cormier measuring trunk.

View of pine on Moxie Road.

crossings on small wooden bridges that can be a tight fit and may be dangerous in high water.

The AT continues on here, coming down from Pleasant Pond Mountain and passing on toward Bald Mountain. If you work out the logistics, a hike could be planned to see this and the spruce on Pleasant Pond Mt. by parking a vehicle at each trailhead. There will be some long driving on dirt roads involved no matter how you decide to get here. We parked off the side of the road and followed the trail across the river.

It was a very dry and a drought year, so the water level may be higher depending on when you go. Patty Cormier, the county forester with me, smelled smoke a short distance up the trail and we found an abandoned campfire that was still smoldering. We went back to her truck and got her water tank, shovel, and grub hoe to put out the fire. I thought we could just dig a little around the campfire and push the smoldering pine needles into the middle, but the fire had burned several inches under the top layer of pine duff. We ended up digging out a 3–4" layer of white ash that was burning pine needles and roots about two extra feet around the fire pit. This could not be seen from above. It could have easily started a forest fire in the area, so we worked hard to put this out by digging out the ash and chopping roots until we were satisfied it would not spread.

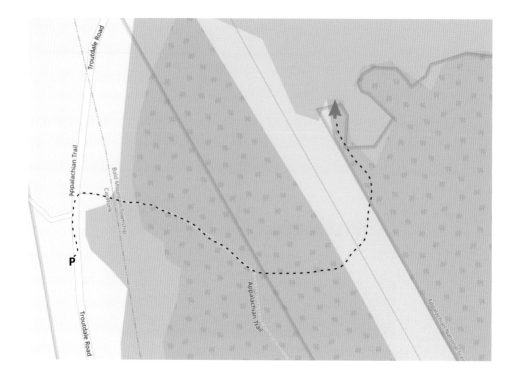

Worn out after this and a grueling earlier hike to find the nearby red spruce, we found the pine without much trouble and felt the impressive tree was worth the effort.

Note the ride to access this tree is on a fifteen-mile-long dirt road in and there are no road signs. Many other dirt roads go off from it, and it may be hard to know which road to go on. Print a map from Google Earth or other sources showing the roads before taking this trip.

Difficulty Rating 3   Long dirt roads, stream crossing. May not be passable in high water.

141" CBH   108' VH   58.5' ACS   Total Points 264   Good Condition
GPS: N 45.25019°   W 069.82857°

Directions

From Route 16 in Moscow, take the dirt Deadwater Road about 10.5 miles and bear left or straight ahead at a fork onto Trestle Road. Go 4.5 miles, and just past a few camps find a place to park near where the AT crosses the road. Walk across the river outlet on the trail to find the tree.

Northern White Cedar *[Thuja occidentalis]*

T his cedar is off the AT in Stratton on the back side of the Bigelow Preserve that borders Flagstaff Lake. Start off by checking out some fair-sized, hemlocks on the south side of Route 16 where the parking area for the trail is located. The kiosk there gives you the lay of the land and was put up by the Maine AT Club, which maintains the trail all through the state. This volunteer organization does incredible work in the tough terrain found in these mountains, so think of them when you see the rock steps and water crossings that help you along the trail. The hemlocks are a few hundred feet down the trail to the

Northern white cedar.

Wood-canvas canoe ribs.

southwest. I picked the largest in circumference and measured its height and crown. The bark does not have as many horizontal chunks as some I have seen, so I think these would be newer growth that came in after a more recent cutting or wind event. A few are to the right of the trail and more up the hill and to the left.

Afterwards, head back towards the parking area and go across the street and follow the AT there to see the cedar. You would be better off using a GPS to find it and then to get back to the trail, but you could find it if stuck without one. Don't get lost, though, and be sure to have a compass and map. Its location along a marked borderline will help. On the way in, you may see several cedars along the trail and several more near the big cedar. Notice how they like the low, wet areas, so when searching for them head downhill toward the water. Could be the fact that they grow near the water that makes the lumber less prone to rot when exposed to the weather. There are several trees between here and the road that have been rubbed by moose cleaning their antlers. I imagine they browse on the small trees near the power lines and the road. The moose would also seek out the road salt if it's used in this area.

White cedar has many names, such as: tree of life, feather leaf, swamp cedar, and eastern arborvitae. The arborvitaes bought to plant around your house are a genetically altered version of this tree. This is an important tree with many uses in the eastern US. I use it for boat and

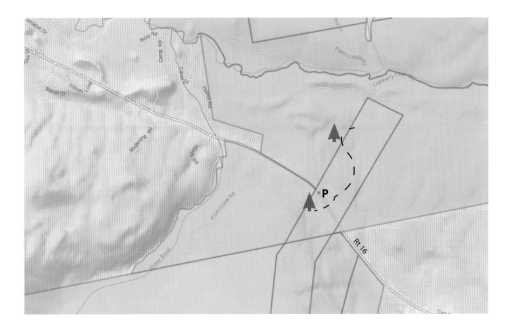

canoe planking and ribs for wood-canvas canoes. It is commonly bought as fencing and fence posts and used for outdoor decking. An oil from the leaves and twigs is used in medicines and perfumes. Northern white cedar is one of my favorite trees, with its bark, leaves, and the ground around it all soft and comfortable-feeling.

I am sure larger cedars can be found in Maine, so if you feel adventurous, a trip to the far northern parts of the state could yield a new state champion for this species. Rocky Brook in Aroostook County has old-growth cedar swamps that have been studied, and one tree was stated to be 43" in diameter in the 1980s, about a ½ mile from the western edge of the township, T13 R10.

Difficulty Rating 3   Off trail use GPS

White Cedar

121" CBH   75' VH   31' ACS   Total Points 204   Fair Condition
GPS: N 45.10677° W 070.35648°

Directions

Take Route 27/16 east out of Stratton toward Sugarloaf ski area 5.25 miles to the parking area for the AT.

Grow Your Own Big Trees

If you have a woodlot and appreciate Big Trees, you may want to get started now on saving some to show off to future generations. It's a rare thing to find a grove of Big Trees, and we should start keeping more of them around. With so many obstacles to prevent a tree from reaching grand size, it's a wonder there are as many as there are. Old age, with its accompanying heart rot and lower resistance to diseases, is one obstacle. Others include the temptation to cut them when of prime size, along with wind, lightening, and insects as natural events. Then we must consider development and homeowner pressures when around population centers.

Most of the Big Trees found now are along boundary lines where the deed may mention them, so the owners keep them around. Some you will see on land that was conserved some time ago and the trees were preserved by the original owners. Old estates in the cities will have those that were planted when the home was built. So, you might consider being that rare landowner that grows them so generations to come can be amazed at their wonder.

To get started, look around at what you have now. If you are lucky enough to have some trees in the three-foot-diameter size-range spread through your lot, then you have a great head start and just need to ask your forester's advice on how to encourage their growth. Most big ones in this area may be pines, and they will make an impressive forest when large, but some hardwoods would add to the landscape. If your lot is further north, your spruce and cedar woods could be turned into a local attraction for those who know those types of trees. Anything from a few acres up would be a great benefit to our grandkids and beyond. You can grow them anywhere as long as they get enough sunlight, but you may want to consider a water source for your really special trees, as most real big ones I have seen have water nearby.

If you are lucky enough to have some old, slow-growing red spruce that you can plan to grow older, future generations can harvest a few here and there when they are ready as tonewood. This is the very valuable and rare wood used in making stringed instruments. The right grain is what makes the good sound in guitars and violins, so it is much sought-after and hard to find. In Europe, they started growing some of these spruces years ago and are able to harvest them, but this country has not, so it would be your chance to start an impressive spruce forest that would have great value. Just be sure to let most of them keep growing to ensure that Big Tree Forest feel.

The Single verses Multi-Stem Dilemma

There is talk of changes in what constitutes a single tree according to the American Forests Big Tree measuring guidelines. While it is clear when you see a single-stem tree with one trunk that it can be measured and entered into the program, when you come across a tree that has several trunks that, upon close inspection, seem to have come from the ground as one tree, things get more difficult.

Formerly, the national measuring guidelines stated that if the tree has no clear separation at ground level, then it could be measured as one tree. Well, sometimes trees just happen to grow close to each other from seeds, and as they get larger, they can meld together close to the ground and still be separate a foot or so up from the ground level. This should be fairly obvious and most would consider them separate trees. Other trees grow close and join together for several feet before showing their separate trunks. You can usually still see a seam where they grew together, and we should consider these as separate also.

Then again, after a tree is cut or otherwise damaged, several sprouts can come out of the stump and grow together over time. This is more difficult to see when the sprouts get larger and no obvious seam is apparent. Some types of trees remain separate, while others, like silver maple, tend to grow together.

As volunteers in the Big Tree Program, those that measure the trees may not have the expertise required to determine if a tree grew from a seed or sprouted as one or several stems. It is left to a best guess at times. In New Hampshire, we have decided to look at the trunks and follow the center or pith line of each trunk, and if they join together above ground level, we consider it one tree. We sometimes measure the several trunks and add them together in a formula that determines their functional circumference as if it is one trunk. On a national level, it is more difficult to get all the states' measurers to agree about that way of measuring.

I have seen pictures of a few national champ trees that are obviously more than one trunk. So, for now there is trouble getting consensus on single- or multiple-stem trees, but some are working to get a change that all can agree to. A national cadre measuring group (of which I am a member) has been formed to follow a set of strict and accurate measuring guidelines on height, crown, and circumference, along with determining if tree is single- or multi-stemmed.

While the different states can determine how to continue measuring their trees to be considered for national champion status, the cadre members, or other trained measurers, would have to measure the tree according to these new guidelines. Let's appreciate the giants of our world for what they are and do our best to follow a fair way to compare and measure a true champion tree.

Massachusetts

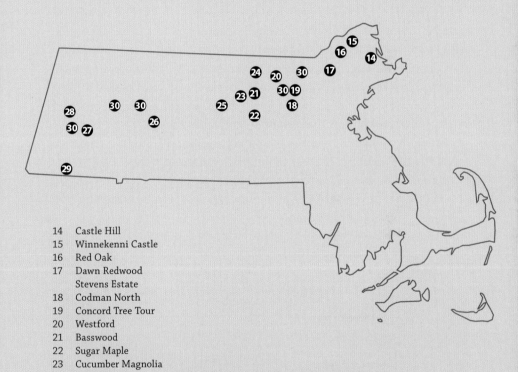

Castle Hill

This is a grand estate of the Chicago industrialist Richard D. Crane, who made a fortune manufacturing pumps, valves, and bathroom fixtures. As with other wealthy estate owners of the early 1900s, his lavish summer retreat included elaborate landscape plantings of exotic trees and awe-inspiring gardens.

Now a National Historic Landmark, Castle Hill is part of the 2,100 acres that include four-mile-long Crane Beach on the ocean front, the Crane Wildlife Refuge of islands, and the salt marsh in the Essex River estuary. There are incredible views all around the hill, with a "grande allée," or promenade, going all the way from the house to the ocean. Over the years, the "Great House," most of the property, and an endowment for its care were turned over to The Trustees, a land trust that has been committed to preserving land and historic places in Massachusetts and keeping it open for public use since 1891.

If you drive in and take the road up to the Great House, keep an eye out along the winding, narrow road for the different types of trees that were planted on the estate. Some of these plantings were started in the late 1800s by the Brown family, who owned it before the mansion was

Casino and mansion on Plum Island Sound.

Garden tower.

built. Other trees were planted when the mansion was built and land-scaped around 1910 to 1912. Not that long ago in tree years, so many of them are not of great size, but some on the property are. Another thing that is noteworthy is the small groves of introduced trees that can be appreciated much more than the single plantings here and there that some estates have. These groves include European beech, European linden, Norway maple, European larch, and Austrian pine.

To start walking to the trees, park in the top parking area and head down toward the Brown cottage, now the Inn at Castle Hill. A trail heads down and you cross the road into the beech grove, which immediately gives you the Old World feeling of Europe with the big, multiple-stem trees that shade and comfort your passage. When the leaves have turned copper, the landscaping value is noticeable as a backdrop to the cottage when first entering the property.

Walk through this grove to the other side, and on the edge of the yard for the cottage will be the biggest tree I saw on the property, a London planetree. This is a cross between the Oriental planetree and the American sycamore, producing a fast-growing and interesting-looking landscape tree with its mottled bark and large, maple-like leaves. The mottled bark continues all the way up, while on the sycamore it turns white on the top half of the trunk.

Continue on the road past the cottage and go right to the farm complex. The buildings here remind one of an Italian villa with its stucco

Larch and arborist Benjamin Carroll.

exteriors and tile roofs. To get a true Old World farm feel, go to the road behind the buildings to see the European lindens that are planted all around, a rare sight in this country. In front of the buildings, you will find the former vegetable garden lot with its ivy-covered towers beckoning you to come closer. The farm buildings that housed animals and the gardens here helped make this a self-sufficient estate when in its prime.

Take the trail through the left-side gate toward the larch that you may have noticed with its drooping boughs of needles that will be green or yellow depending on the season. The trail goes through some larches and past a line of Norway maples. These trees are not highly thought of by some foresters, who have had to fight the spread of these prolific trees in woods they have managed.

Continue along this trail that goes around the outskirts of the property and soon you will come to a large Austrian pine. Also called black pine, this dark tree is larger than any I have seen in New Hampshire, and there are not any listed in Massachusetts to compare it to. Even though I have seen a larger one in Maine, this is significant in the area for this type of tree.

As you continue along the trail, keep an eye out for wildlife. I saw a doe and two fawns watch me in surprise from a short distance away as I rounded a corner and then disappear into the brush. You will notice that as with many old coastal properties, the land that was once open is now covered with many invasive shrubs that make it hard to walk off-trail and are smothering some of the trees. Although they provide cover for the wildlife, they also are a concern and should be dealt with.

It is very labor intensive to remove the invasives, and it can be difficult to find the funds required. The Trustees have been spending a lot of time and effort renewing the gardens and planting new trees to replace those lost in wind storms of the past. At some point, they may get to ridding the property of some of these overpowering plants. For now, they do provide cover for the deer, some turkeys, and I'm sure many birds and small mammals that hide from the hawks that were circling overhead.

Make your way around and bear right toward Steep Beach to the large larch just in the woods on the right before the trail junction and the very large silver maple next to the restrooms on the next trail to the left.

Difficulty Rating 2

1. London Planetree

163" C   85' VH   58' ACS   Total Points 262   Excellent Condition
GPS: N 42.684364° W 70.776816°

2. Austrian Pine

87" C   60' VH   42' ACS   Total Points 157   Fair Condition
GPS N 42.684878° W 70.783673°

3. European Larch

116" C   80' VH   42' ACS   Total Points 204   Good Condition
GPS N 42.684878° W 70.783673°

4. Silver Maple

193" C   80' VH   74' ACS   Total Points 285   Good Condition
GPS N 42.690307° W 70.778774°

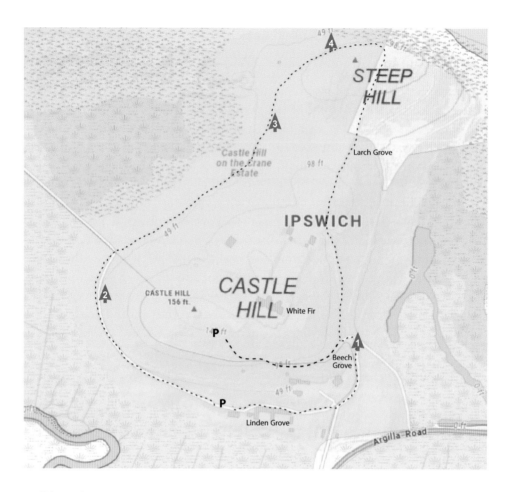

Directions

From Route 1A in Ipswich, take Argilla Road and go 4 miles to the entrance to the Castle on Crane Hill. Entrance fee is charged.

Winnekenni Park

This impressive, small castle was built in 1875 and was sold to the city of Haverhill in 1895. The building was boarded up in the 1960s until a group was formed to manage it as a venue for special events. The park now consists of more than two hundred acres surrounding Kenoza Lake. Many of the original trees planted when the castle was built are on the road in and up near the castle. The surrounding native trees grew in as the fields and open grounds grew in over the years. You can see a statue of a stag deer, a magnificent fountain, the remains of another old estate with its European beech and the Dudley Porter memorial bench at the lakefront. There are several good-sized

Cucumber magnolia.

European larch growing here, and I measured what turns out to be the largest magnolia in the state. Other notable trees include the many black oaks and some special cedars near the second parking area.

You could make this an easy walk by parking at the bottom parking area and walking up the road to the castle, but I would suggest a few alternatives that would bring you to the castle at the end of either a hike around the Basin and then along Kenoza Lake before going up to the castle, or a hike on Plug Pond Trail to the pond then up the trail along the back side of the hill near some of the Birchbrow Estate remains of stone walls, other small stone structures, and some European beech. The alternative of going around the Basin brings you to the lakeshore with its views, so I will describe that here. Go north from the parking area toward the entrance and Route 110 and follow the walkway there past a playground. On the other side of the Basin, you take a right up a knoll where you will see some hickories, locust, oaks, and other trees to keep your identification skills up to date.

On the bottom of the other side of the hill, you may notice the Carlton Fountain, which is worth a side trip to see, or keep going to the Dudley Porter Trail and either go up to the castle or follow along the lake a while longer and take Castle Trail just past the Dudley Porter bench. Castle Trail is a sharp right where you start going up-hill to the castle. Black oak seems to dominate some areas along this trail. A selective cutting was going on near the castle in 2019, so you may see signs of the logging work, which should blend in more after a few years. When the castle was built, the land was all open, with great views of the surrounding lake and ponds. The forestry work has opened some of the views back up and will add to the great experience when visiting here.

Once you start approaching the area around the castle, keep a lookout for the cucumber magnolia. It will be the tree with the biggest circumference and is near the small buildings in the wooded area. This magnolia will show white flowers in the spring, then green, cucumber-like fruit in the early summer that changes to purple seed pods in the fall. Look for the mottled, brownish-tan bark to help ID the tree.

I am assuming this tree was planted when the castle was built and is around 145 years old. Compare the growth rate of this to the nearby larches, which are considerably smaller but likely planted at the same time. This may help you become impressed when seeing those trees that are old and big for their type but just can't reach a great size.

Start wandering around and check out the nearby larches planted

Red-tailed hawk.

around the grounds. They must look spectacular in the different seasons with their bright-green needles and purple flowers in the spring turning to a golden-yellow in the fall before becoming bare for the winter. Even the stark winter tree brings out the impressive gray stonework of the Winnikenni Castle. The biggest in circumference is the lone larch on the other side of the castle. It's not a champion tree, but its size is comparable to some of the biggest I have measured in New Hampshire.

Work your way down the hill behind the castle toward Plug Pond on the right if you're going back the way you came on Castle Trail. Keep bearing right to follow Plug Pond Trail back toward where you parked. Keep an eye out for birds and other wildlife. We saw the reddish tail of a red-tailed hawk fly low into the tree branches but take off again before I had time to get a picture. The second time I visited, the hawk seemed to follow me from the nearby cemetery where it was high in the air while I measured a tuliptree. When I pulled up to the top of the hill at the castle, it landed in the top of the big larch I measured earlier and posed for some photos. I guess that means I should associate this spot with the red-tailed hawk.

Some good black oak trees are throughout the area, and you will come to a lone American elm. The other trees to see are a row of cedars

Larch and the castle.

near the dirt parking area and bordering Castle Road. These could have been planted as a windbreak for visitors that met here at this road junction or for their appealing looks before heading up to the castle.

You are sure to be impressed by this great property with all its history, waterfront, hilltop views, and Big Trees.

Difficulty Rating 2

European Larch

105" CBH   70.5' VH   45.3' ACS   Total Points 186   Good Condition
GPS: N 42.788650°   W 071.063645°

Cucumber Magnolia

151" CBH   88' VH   63' ACS   Total Points 254   Good Condition
GPS: N 42.788124°   W 071.062550°
Δ State Champion

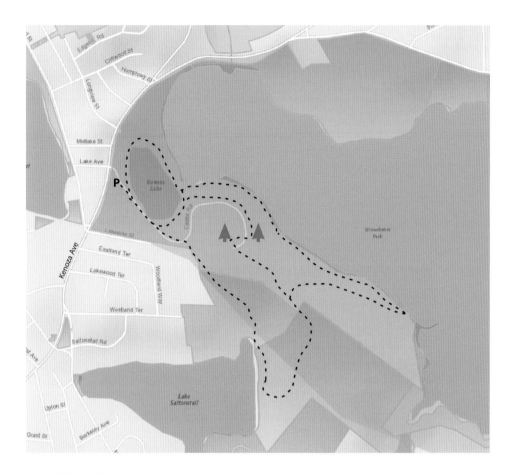

Directions

From I-495, take Exit 52 to Kenoza Avenue or Route 110 west toward Haverhill, about ¾ of a mile to Winnekenni Park entrance, just after Lake Kenoza on the left.

It can get busy and parking may be full on weekends or holidays. Download maps and see info at the City of Haverhill website.

Red Oak *[Quercus rubra]*

I f you want to bring young children on a short hike to see a Big Tree, then Tattersall Farm in Haverhill would work out great. There is a slide at the parking area, some tractors and farm implements for them to see up close, a community garden, and a not-too-long walk through the fields and woods. You cross a small shallow stream on planks a few times and end up at an oak that is sure to command their attention for a few minutes. If it's winter, any fresh snow is likely to have tracks of wildlife

Red oak.

that visit the fields and the area right around the tree. We saw deer and possum tracks leading right up to the tree.

The trail back goes through the woods and a few swampy areas. You have to keep an eye out and be sure to follow the red arrow trail markers, some of which are painted on the trees. There are several trail junctions that require you to look at your map (available online) to be sure you go the right way. If the kids get tired or cranky, it might be easier to take the field back the way you came.

Red oak is a hard and heavy wood that has many uses. I have some in my living room that my brother and I rolled up on log ramps onto a 3'-high, 8'-long homemade trailer using a rope wrapped around the trunk and pulling from the trailer with one of us on a log roller working it up the ramps. These were trees that blew over in a straight-line wind in Stratham, New Hampshire, and I was asked if I wanted them. One was over 2' in diameter and had perfectly clear wood for about 20 feet. We got it on the trailer, but it weighed the trailer down so much we had to cut it to about 12' to get it to the sawmill. We had it cut into 1" boards, then brought it to someone who milled it into tongue-and-groove flooring for our living rooms.

Looking at this tree, you can see that it was open-grown at one time, and the woods grew in around it later. The lower branches died as the smaller trees grew in around it, shading those branches, and they will soon fall off. The top looks pretty good, as the leaves have stayed above the surrounding growth. If the tree had grown at the same time as the surrounding forest, it would have a straight and clear trunk for some distance before branching. It and many of the nearby trees would be about the same size unless some wind event or thinning during a cut removed some of them. Hillside trees also commonly grow straight and tall trying to reach the sunlight as it comes over the hill. Other trees at cemeteries or old estates may have been pruned of their lower branches when they were young. As a boatbuilder, I look for those long straight trunks in hopes that they provide good clear lumber. There is a nearby stream providing a good water source that has helped this tree grow to its large size.

Difficulty Rating 1

186" CBH 78' VH 68' ACS Total Points 281 Fair to Good Condition
GPS: N 42.792839° W 71.128526°

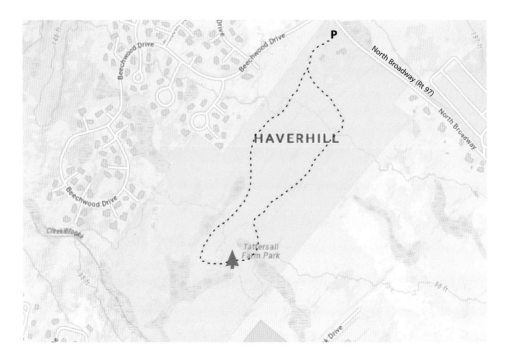

Directions

From Route 125 in the center of Haverhill, take Route 97 (Broadway) 1.5 miles to a right turn onto North Broadway. Follow that another 1.5 miles to Tattersall Farm on your left.

Dawn Redwood *[Metasequoia glyptostroboides]*

This type of tree was thought extinct until they were found deep in the woods of China in the early 1940s. This caused much excitement in the forestry community, and cuttings or seeds were brought to the US and Europe to try to introduce the species into those areas. This tree is known to have existed in the US over two million years ago, because fossilized remains have been found on the West Coast. These findings were considered significant enough that Oregon declared them the state fossil. Many test plantings of the Chinese samples were done on the East Coast, with the Arnold Arboretum in Boston taking the lead in conducting extensive studies on the species. You can see some now in the Arboretum and at sites across the Northeast.

This significant sample was likely planted in the 1940s, and the

Dawn redwood.

Legacy beech tree off Osgood Hill Trail.

fast-growing species has already grown to Big Tree size. We have yet to see the size they will reach in the US, but they likely will not reach the great size of the giant redwoods on the West Coast; the largest of those seed trees found in China were about 160' tall and up to 7' diameter.

See the redwood and a European larch at the Stevens-Coolidge place right off Andover Street in North Andover. This property, now owned and managed by The Trustees, is kept as an example of an early 1800s country retreat, with updates to the home and landscaping by Boston architect Joseph Chandler in the early 1900s. You can walk the grounds from 8 a.m. to sunset, but the home is only open for special events, so you may want to time your tree tour for one of those events days.

1. Dawn Redwood

182"C 95' VH 51' ACS Total Points 289 Excellent Condition
GPS: N 42.68127° W 071.11901°

2. European Larch

114" CBH 78' VH 38' ACS Total Points 201 Good Condition
GPS: N 42.68142° W 071.11816°

Difficulty Rating: 1 for Coolidge Stevens; 2 for Stevens Estate; 3 if walking to both.

Stevens Estate

If just checking the trees, there is not much of a hike involved at the Stevens-Coolidge House and Gardens, so I have added the nearby Stevens Estate to this chapter. You can drive a few miles down the road to the estate, or, to make a day of it, they now have walking trails that connect the sites. Once at the estate, you will see some impressive beech trees with a European version in front of the main building and the American version along the Osgood Hill Trail that has what they call legacy trees marked near the lake. Park near the carriage house and take the Stevens Trail (green markers) down to a seating area on the shore of Lake Coch-ichewick, then follow the lake shore on the right along the Osgood Hill Trail (orange markers) and you soon come to a sign showing the legacy trees and their diameters. Start looking for #3, which is an American beech that is a little off the trail and surrounded by younger growth. The large, long, straight trunk shows no signs of the disease effecting other beech, and this example is one of the largest I have seen in Mass. I will have to associate this site with the gray squirrel, as in the big nut year I visited there were a few dozen seen along the trails.

Follow the trail along the lakeshore and skirt the hill until you get close to the top, then look for a side trail that comes out to the field. There is seating at the top of the hill with a nice view of the lake and a pignut hickory that is separated in its own island just into the field. Head back into the woods from the seating and take the Summit Trail (red markers) back down to the parking area. From there walk over to the brick mansion and visit with the large European version of the beech with its leaves draping down to give romantic views of the building through its branches.

Difficulty Rating: 1 for Coolidge Stevens; 2 for Stevens Estate; 3 if walking to both.

3. American Beech

105" CBH   94' VH   50' ACS   Total Points 211   Excellent Condition
GPS: N 42.71022°   W 71.10712°

Directions

From North Andover, take Massachusetts Avenue 1.5 miles to a right on Osgood Street past the town green to a right on Andover Street and look for the Coolidge Stevens place on your right. Park across the street on Chestnut Street in the parking area.

Note that there is limited access on weekends and you must preregister to visit then. You may want to call for their policy in the future: (978) 689-9105.

To get to the Stevens Estate, go back on Andover Street to Osgood Street and follow it, bearing right at the fork of Main Street, staying on Osgood 1.75 miles to the estate on the right.

Codman North Hemlock

I think of the hemlock tree as a dweller of dark woods and cool valleys but feel warm and comforted when under their boughs. In fact, they do provide warmth and comfort for many wildlife creatures, and in a pinch, those with low branches offer us a great shelter from a winter storm. Quite common throughout the Northeast, they will be seen mixed in with oaks and pines but can become the dominant species when the chance arises. Hemlocks can survive well in the shade, so younger hemlocks flourish under the larger ones and prevent less shade-tolerant trees from growing. When the larger hemlock dies, the undergrowth spurts up to replace the big one. Some of these smaller trees can be very old and are just waiting for the chance to grow larger. Groves of hemlocks will be dominant until something like a fire or clear-cut allows other types of trees to grow in.

The trail at the Codman Estate begins at the parking area as you enter the property and your walk brings you past the front of the house. Keep an eye open for what type of trees you can see planted around the

Codman Estate.

ground. Some were planted as frames for the views of the fields that were at one time part of the estate, but now much of the acreage has been split up and is managed by different groups, including the farming properties seen while driving the road in. Sixteen acres of the main grounds, along with the house, was turned over to the Historic New England Properties in 1968. They manage it as a home of historic significance and maintain the house and grounds for the public to view. The grounds are open for no charge, and, if you want to see the interior of the home, a fee helps them keep up the good work. The northern woods section was turned over to the Town of Lincoln, and they keep it as undeveloped recreational land, called Codman North, with the Bay Circuit Trail passing through the property.

Follow the gravel path around the backside of the house, and to the right you will see a multi-trunk hemlock whose main trunk is massive by itself. This would surely be a champion if measured according to the old guidelines where these multiple trunks would be measured at 4.5 ft. or the narrowest point between the trunks and the root flare. Using the newer requirements, I measured the biggest of the trunks around at 138" CBH and the height is 95'. Its open-grown branches hang down low, so you have to go under them to see the trunks. You certainly get that sheltered feel with this behemoth. Another asset for these heavily branched trees is the ability to climb them, not that you should climb this one. I have one in my front yard that has taught my children and my grandchildren the fine art of tree climbing with the many branches to grab while climbing and providing the relative feeling of safety to a parent or grandparent that, if they slip, the many branches will break their fall.

Get back on the gravel path and follow it past the side of the back building and over to the railroad tracks. Here you can see an alternate way to get here, starting from the parking area at Lincoln Station (a parking fee may be charged) and following the other side of the track and crossing the pedestrian bridge. You will likely see and hear the trains go by a few times while on your jaunt to this tree. Bear left on this side of the bridge to continue along the tracks a bit and down into the woods. You will start seeing some larger oaks and hemlocks as you walk along, and as you get to the end of these woods look to the right down near the wet area that might provide the water the biggest of these trees need to grow. Here is where you will find the largest circumference hemlock of these woods. Close up, it will impress with its rough bark and large roots

Old-looking hemlock.

disappearing into the ground. I will associate this tree with the hawk, as I thought I heard one while around it, then when sighting the top for the height measurement a hawk was circling high in the sky. I tried to point the rangefinder at it to see how high it was but the raptor was too far up to take a reading. This special spot in Lincoln with these big hemlocks gives the feel of the old forests without going too far off the beaten path.

Difficulty Rating 1

140" CBH   100' VH   43' ACS   Total Points 251   Good Condition
GPS: N 42.42023°   W 071.33345°

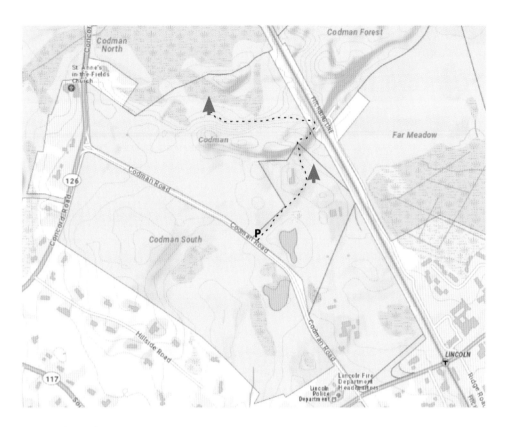

Directions

From I-95, take Trapelo Road about 2.5 miles to the end in Lincoln then go left on Lincoln Road. Bear right at the fork staying on Lincoln Road for 1.6 miles and go right onto Codman Road. Go 0.3 miles to parking at the entrance to the Codman Estate on the right.

Concord Tree Tour

The Minuteman National Park has plenty of history and gives you a sense of what it was like during the American Revolution. Much of the fighting was done in the woods and likely from behind some of the Big Trees in those woods. Around the North Bridge Visitors Center would be a good place to start looking at the trees, with a river birch right behind the stone wall near the road out front. Some good-sized pin oak and beech can be seen near the building. You may want to go in the Visitors Center and get a lay of the land then take a walk on the trail out to the Minuteman statue, the Old Manse, with a stone boathouse on the Concord River, and a nice swamp white oak next to the boat house.

First, go out front to see the river birch that is near the road. It is the nicest looking of the birches, with graceful branches and leaves that hang down similar to the weeping willow. When older like this one, the bark is much more like what you see on a cherry than other types of birches, but if you see the younger trees, the tan, paper-like curling bark is unmistakable. Most of these trees are planted, although they are

Swamp white oak and boathouse.

natural to the southern New England area. The unusual-looking bark and graceful branches make this a sought-after ornamental, and the trees I have seen were mostly planted in parks and at homes or businesses. I have seen birch frequently used on the decks and thwarts of the old wood and canvas canoes. I like to think it is river birch, but I have never taken the steps to confirm whether it is or not. Most likely, it's the more commonly used yellow birch. The Latin name for this tree is *Betula nigra*, which means black birch, but it is not the same tree as what is called black birch in most of New England. That tree is *Betula lenta*, which means sweet birch. The confusion with common names is one reason why most foresters and botanists will use the Latin name when writing reports on trees or other plants.

Head past the Visitors Center and out on the gravel trail and across the bridge to the Minuteman Monument and on to the other parking area on the right, where there is a nice ash and Norway spruce worth looking at. Then go to the Old Manse, which was once the home of American writers Ralph Waldo Emerson and then Nathaniel Hawthorn. It was turned over to the Trustees of Reservations in 1939. The Trustees was established in 1891 for the purposes of acquiring, holding, maintaining, and opening to the public historic and beautiful places in Massachusetts. This early start in conserving properties around the state has allowed the Trustees to set aside an amazing amount of land and historic buildings for the public to enjoy. The Old Manse with its great oak is just one of them. The grounds are open for no fee but consider helping the organization continue its good work by visiting the house and paying the admission fee or better yet become a member of the Trustees.

After checking out the house, go around back on the trail that leads to the boathouse and a large swamp white oak in a perfect setting near the river. An 1895 photo stationed near the entrance shows the tree almost as large then as it is now. During my second visit here, the scene was the backdrop for filming of the movie *Little Women*, and I had to give way from measuring the tree to the actresses and film crew who for some reason did not want me in the movie. Nice wooden Rangeley and St. Lawrence skiff rowboats were in the water, and they were rowing them past the boat house. Some of the white oak ribs in those boats may have come from the same type of tree. It could also be that this particular tree inspired some of the great writings of those that lived here.

If you want to walk the same routes that the famous naturalists Henry David Thoreau and Ralph Waldo Emerson followed, then walking on to see Concord's massive white pine is right up your alley. Not far from Walden Pond, the original seventy-eight acres of the Hapgood Wright Town Forest was bought in 1935 with funds given to the town of Concord in 1885 in honor of its 250th birthday. The $1000 gift was to be invested for fifty years, then could be spent for the improvement of the town. Later additions to the property were made possible through fundraising efforts of Don Henley of the Eagles fame, along with many others, in a nationwide campaign when the Walden Woods were threatened with development. This pine was likely big enough to be noticed by Thoreau and Emerson in their days and continues to help us ponder the wonders of nature today.

To visit this tree, go to the front of the Old Manse and go right or south on Monument Street about a ½ mile to Monument Square. Turn left past the monument and into downtown Concord with all its shops and eateries. From there, walk down Walden Street and take a left on Haywood Street to Haywood Meadows. You can then catch the Emerson Thoreau Amble Trail, which is also part on the Bay Circuit Trail. On the trail, go past the Emerson House out to Walden Street and follow some field edges, then go back to the woods and along Clintonia Swamp until it meets the yellow-blazed trail. Head left past the Hapgood Monument and then left again at Fairyland Pond to get to the tree.

There are good maps of the site available online that will help you stay along the marked trail. At the end of the pond, take the spur trail to the right that follows the edge of Clintonia Swamp and the steep hillside to the right. You may notice a few fair-sized hardwoods along the hillside, and before you know it, the pine will show up on the swamp side. An impressive pine it is, with the old-growth bark and a good girth. The most impressive part is its height of almost 140', which may make it the tallest tree in this part of the state. The hillside trees nearby compete with it, so this pine needs to keep getting taller to reach that sunlight coming up on the eastern side of the property. There is also the extra water getting pulled up from the swamp, helping it reach its maximum growth. While looking this tree over, keep your eyes and ears open for the birds and other wildlife in this swamp, which I'm sure is a haven for them in an area that is near the big city development of Boston.

When done, head back to the pond the way you came and across the outlet to the pond where the new type of barrier is set up to prevent beavers from damming up the pond. This is a never-ending battle at times, and I saw some branches that the beavers were trying to set in place

Thoreau likely noticed this pine while wandering the area.

around the barrier. While these mammals are beneficial to wildlife with the wetlands they create, as each generation comes along, the offspring look for new sites to build their own dam and home, which can create problems with flooding when near developed areas.

Stay right on the yellow trail past a monument set in stone that recognizes Hapgood Wright, who made the conservation of the land possible, then go right again to follow the trail back to Haywood Meadows. You can break up the walk back with lunch and a little shopping before ending this significant trip through Big Tree history.

Difficulty Rating 2   For distance.

River Birch

120" CBH   51' VH   48' ACS   Total Points 183   Fair Condition
GPS: N 42.471638°   W 71.353622°

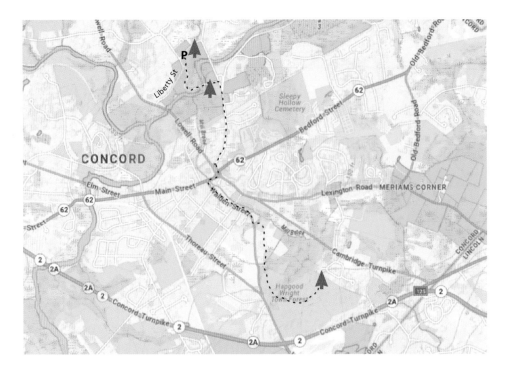

Swamp White Oak

172" CBH   74' H   88' ACS   Total Points 268   Good Condition
GPS: N 42.38033°   W 71.35040°

Eastern White Pine

157" CBH   137' VH   56' ACS   Total Points 308   Good Condition
GPS: N 42.451158°   W 71.337056°

Directions

From Concord, go to the end of Main Street and left on Route 62 just before Monument Square. Go a little over a ½ mile to a right on Liberty Street, then up to the entrance for the national park. There is no fee to walk the grounds and Minuteman Road, but you can pay a fee to see interior of the homes on group tours. It can get busy, so you may have to find alternate parking over by the Old Manse or in the downtown area. You could also start the walk from the other end at the parking area for Hapgood Wright Town Forest on Walden St. across from the high school.

Westford

T ake a trip to this small town and see the state champion black oak and shagbark hickory. A combination of the small-town atmosphere around the black oak and the conserved woodland where the hickory is located will make it worthwhile.

Westford is a suburban town close to Lowell and right off the 495 turnpike. Early homeowners living here worked in the Lowell Mills, while, more recently, many residents traveled to Boston and high-tech firms along Route 128 for work. Now many tech firms and corporate

Black oak from the commons.

offices are located here. Westford Academy was established in 1793 as a private school that later turned into the public high school it is now. Paul Revere's son attended the academy, and a bell he cast sits in the lobby of the school. He also made the weathervane that graces the top of the Abbott Elementary School in town. As an older town, there is a lot to see in the form of history and architecture, much of which is within short walking distance. Start out by parking behind the library or at the town hall. Work your way over to the J. V. Fletcher Library, and on the side toward the church you will see the Massachusetts state champion black oak. The massive trunk has a fence around it to help protect the roots. Hovering over the library roof, it is the most noticeable natural feature that you will see while standing in the commons.

Black oak is often seen in this part of Mass, but most people think of it just as an oak or as the more common red oak. I can see some difference in the bark of this tree, with coarser and darker bark compared to the giant red oaks. The acorns will have more of a cap on them and the twigs will have hairy, yellowish buds compared to the smooth, reddish buds of red oak.

Walk across the street to the commons and view this tree from a town perspective and you can appreciate why many towns, including this one, love their Big Trees. We should encourage town officials to work to keep them around in any way they can. This tree looks quite healthy and is probably protected by the buildings from some of the prevailing winds in this location. One of the reasons we lose many of our big trees is because of their location in the wide open with no trees surrounding them, as they may have had in a forested setting. In the forest, the trees are supported by one another as the wind blows them in a group instead of individually, as in an open setting. This is why many times when a clearing is cut in a forest, some trees bordering the cut will be lost to wind damage until new growth provides support.

If you want to continue walking to the hickory, go across the commons toward the Civil War statue and Hildereth Street. Use caution on the short walk down the street to Prospect Hill and the conservation land. There are no sidewalks, and the road can get busy with traffic. Just past 11 Hildereth Street, you will see a gate, and if you take that into the field, a trail will take you to the left toward the woods on the far end of the field. When entering the woods, notice the many smaller Norway spruce growing naturally here. They must have spread from a nearby planting around an old estate or house. These trees are an example of

State champ shagbark hickory.

why American Forests accepts this species in the Big Tree Program as a naturalized tree in the United States. Some introduced species will not reproduce on their own in this country, while others will. They only accept trees that will grow naturally.

Work your way to the right at the fields end and follow the yellow trail markers around the edge of the property and up to the highest point in town. You can see the water tower on the bordering town land at the top that gravity-feeds water down to the residents. The trail is not long, so when going down the hill, keep an eye out toward the road and the state's biggest shagbark hickory will show itself rather quickly.

This hickory is a bit different in the fact that the roots have grown against the large rock next to it and the tree seems to be using the rock as a brace against the winds. This is the largest of the type I have seen in the four northern New England states. An important tree for its nuts, it also produces strong and durable lumber. Farmers would use it for the bottoms of their log skids, and it is well-known as a durable wood for hammer and ax handles. I will associate this hickory with bats. Most bat species will use trees with loose bark to hide under and stay warm. Eastern red bats require taller, more mature trees to roost in. These are the trees that get more sunlight, which is important to keep bat pups warm while raising them. Bats will roost in the outer canopy and move as needed according to the sun and wind to stay warm or to cool off.

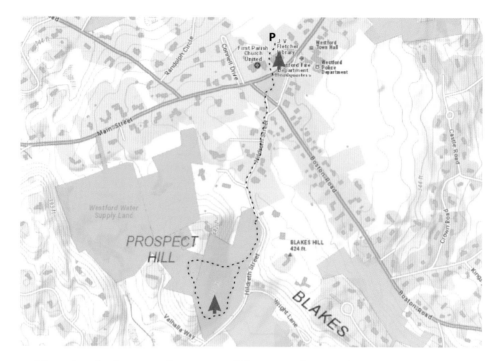

I imagine the bats use this tree and fly out to the nearby roads and fields to catch insects. Since they are long-lived and do not have more than a few pups in a season, we have to keep many of these larger trees around for them to survive. One more reason to appreciate Big Trees.

Difficulty Rating 2 Traffic on road.

Black Oak

236" C   81.5' VH   98' ACS   Total Points 342   Fair Condition
GPS: N 42.58167°   W 071.43887°
Δ State Champion

Shagbark Hickory

146' CBH   85' VH   76' ACS   Total Points 250   Good Condition
GPS: N 42.57474°   W 071.44054°
Δ State Champion

Directions

From I-495, take Boston Road north 1 mile to Main Street and turn right. Go to the end of the town green and you will see the library on the left. Park behind the library.

Basswood *[Tilia americana L.]*

Basswood is a tree that I see sporadically in the woods of northern New England. This isn't because it does not grow in the area but because when you do come across this type of tree there will likely be only one or two in the property. The flowers and then fruit are attached to long, leaf-like bracts that slow the seeds' fall to the ground and allow the wind to carry them out from under the shade of the parent tree. You may see them scattered on the ground all around the base. They do not travel far and lie dormant until passed through a mouse or chipmunk who will eat the seeds. Apparently, they do not go far as these trees are not widespread. They germinate poorly, and the fact that they grow readily by sprouting must account for the trees not growing very far from the parent tree area.

The tree has gray, lightly furrowed bark with intersecting ridges that get deeper on older trees. The leaves can get big as your hand, very large compared to the European linden that is more often planted around houses and town centers. It flowers in early summer, attracting bees of all sorts to gather its nectar. In the past, people would gather and dry the flowers for tea to relieve anxiety and irregular heartbeat, or as a fragrance for bathwater that is said to quell hysteria.

The wood is light for a hardwood and somewhat fuzzy when working and finishing. I have used it for wider floorboards in some of the canoes that call for two-piece floors. The basswood will not crack when stepped on compared to the spruce or pine that is normally used for narrower floorboards. I carved some hollow, wood-duck decoys made of glued-up blocks of basswood. Nice and light, but still rugged. I have also used the wood to carve carrying yokes and for the sideboards on an old sleigh. It's a very stable wood, so was cut into wide boards called whitewood and used to build carriage and sleigh sides.

This tree is at the Weatherby Cemetery in the Old Town Center historic district of Boxborough. Basswood was often planted because of the dense foliage that makes it one of the best shade trees for parks and other public areas. The town center includes the site of the former meeting

house built in 1775 (burned down in 1953). You can see the granite foundation with the partly burned tower bell on display out front.

To make a hike out of this visit, you can start by parking on Barteau Lane at the end of the road. The property here is called the Have Not Pond Conservation Area, and a map is available on the town website. Walk along the open fields and bear left following the red trail through the fields and eventually into the wood line and a woods road to meet the Yellow Trail. If you take a left here, it will bring you around and back out to an access trail back to Hill Road past the schoolhouse. If you go straight or right, you can take the shorter trail out to Schoolhouse Road or catch another access trail to Hill Road. If you want to see the schoolhouse after exiting this access trail you would have to walk up (north) Hill Road. From the schoolhouse, you go back down (south) on Hill Road a little over half a mile to the cemetery and the tree. A shorter option is to go right between the two ponds from the red trail off Barteau Lane and go over a wooden bridge to the woods on the other side. The trail bears right along an old tote road. You will soon see some granite pillars at the top of a steep slope on the left. That is the back of the cemetery. Continue on the trail up to another parking area where you can go left a short way along the road up to the cemetery and the tree. Near the parking area, you will notice some unusual looking trees that are called trees of heaven, a non-native tree that seems to be spreading as an invasive in some areas of Massachusetts. I have not seen them in New Hampshire, but they are likely there also. All these trails can also be followed by starting at this parking area on Hill Road.

I will associate this site with robins, as we saw small flock of them eating the berries off some nearby shrubs on the late-January day we visited. Some bluebirds were mixed in as they all flew in and out of the basswood.

Difficulty Rating 2

149" C   78.5' H   66.5' ACS   Total Points 244   Good Condition
GPS: N 42.491741° W 71.527264°

◄ *Basswood in old town center.*

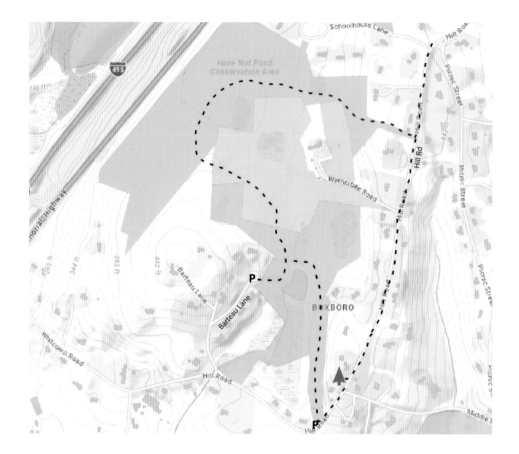

Directions

From Route 111 in Boxborough, take Middle Road to the end, then turn left on Hill Road and look for a parking area on the right just before a curve in the road. To make a hike out of it, drive further down Hill Road and take a right at Barteau Lane and follow it to the end, bearing right to a parking area. This can be a long walk through the woods and back along Hill Road from the old schoolhouse to the tree. Or you can go a shorter route walking from Barteau Lane to the parking area on Hill Road, then on to the tree.

Sugar Maple *[Acer saccharum]*

We all know the sugar maple trees that stand in front of many old farmhouses with hanging sap buckets signaling the start of spring in the Northeast. Its wide crown and yellow leaves also make it the classic tree to see when doing your fall leaf-peeping.

Mount Ward has a trail that starts out on a gas pipeline cut and then goes into the woods and around the backside of this hill, which is called a mountain for some reason. The map that you can download online says it has the greatest elevation changes of all the conserved land in the area. I guess its steepness in areas makes it seem like a mountain. The trail goes down near a small stream where there are some yellow birch growing around this cooler niche of the woods. Continue around the backside of the hill and you will see some eastern hophornbeam as you

Sugar maple on the top of Mount Ward.

get to the higher ground. There are many small ones here and a few that are fair-sized for this type. As you go up look for the pignut hickories spread all along the stone wall. Near the top, the Big Tree mentioned in the trail map starts to show itself. Although not real big for its type, it's good-sized and sitting in a great spot with a commanding presence on the top of the hill.

I don't have much experience working with sugar or "hard" maple lumber. Its use in boat work is limited. Maple is used for Adirondack guideboat oars and canoe paddles, but the hard maple is heavier and harder to carve than the red or silver "soft" maple, so I use the soft maple. Furniture makers seem to prefer the hard maple. I imagine flooring and countertops made from it would wear longer, too. The sap from the sugar maple has been a staple for people to use in flavoring meals ever since someone in the long ago past noticed the insects drawn to the sap dripping from a wound in a tree and then tasted its sweet flavor. Maple syrup is an industry in itself with many farmers getting an early start with agricultural products by selling the sweet syrup to the many waiting buyers.

Difficulty Rating 2

149" CBH   76' VH   48' ACS   Total Points 237   Fair Condition
GPS: N 42.355954°   W 71.497393°

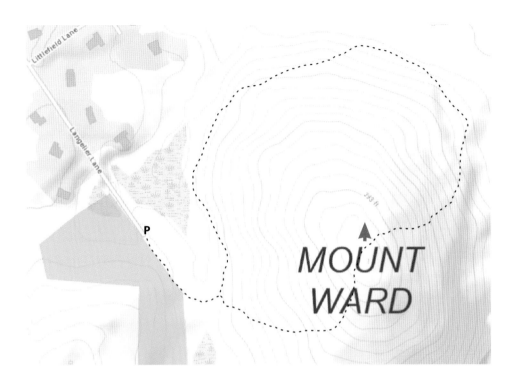

Directions

From the junction with Route 85, take Route 20 East for 2.4 miles out of Marlboro. Turn left onto Wilson Street and follow it to its junction with Hemmingway Street, turn right and go a short distance to Langelier Street, then turn right. Follow Langelier to the end and park. The trail for Mount Ward starts from there.

Cucumber Magnolia *[Magnolia acuminata]*

Northborough is home for this special tree that is normally not viewed in northern New England unless it was planted in someone's yard. Its normal range in the wild includes southern Appalachia up to New York and into southern Ontario. Newer native range maps for the type shows it growing in several counties in Mass, but this site is likely as far northeast as it has progressed on its own. The warming trend is allowing some species to grow more readily in northern New England and maybe these types of trees will start growing to large sizes into New Hampshire as the climate gets more hospitable to the magnolia's needs. They do spread readily, though, and it is said that this likely came from tree a planted in a cemetery nearby at the gravesite of Cyrus Scale. It must have started some time ago to gain the size of this beauty that is special to see in this part of the country within a wooded setting. The Edmunds Hill Woods property that it is on was set aside to be kept in a wild state by Edwin Proctor in 1967. A diverse forest exists here with chestnut sprouts, sassafras, hickories, beech, pines, oaks, maples, and magnolia. I even found a holly on the spur trail past the magnolia. The impressive oaks and pines along the trails show the results of a proper cutting of the forest in earlier years. Lots of wildlife are found in these woods, with many birds and frogs making noise in early October and a deer moving away from me further up the hill.

Magnolia in woods setting.

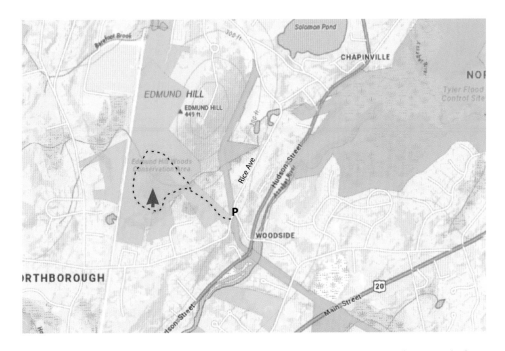

The cucumber magnolia is recognizable by its rough, mottled, brownish bark, the larger oblong leaves, and most noticeably its cucumber shaped fruit. The fruit is green into the early summer and turns purple later in the year with bright red-orange seeds bulging out. Its greenish yellow, tulip-like flowers that bloom high up in the tree are not noticeable in the in the spring, but the fruit can be seen in the fall and litters the ground around the tree. Some of the local wildlife must eat the fruit, and I hope will help spread the species. The lumber from the tree is said to be mixed with the lumber of a close relative the tuliptree and commonly sold as poplar.

Difficulty Rating 1 to 2

102" CBH   111' VH   48' ACS   Total Points 225   Excellent Condition
GPS: N 42.33145° W 071.63739°
Δ Former State Champion

Directions

From Route 20 in Northborough, take Hudson St. about 1 mile to a left on Allen St. Follow that to the junction with Rice Ave. and the parking area is across the street at the corner. From the I-495 exit, take Route 20 toward Northborough for 2.2 miles to a right on N Main Street. Follow ½ mile to a right on Allen Street to end at Rice Avenue.

Paper birch.

Paper Birch *[Betula papyrifera]*

D rive over to the Far and Near Reservation if you want an easy viewing of the largest recorded paper birch in Massachusetts. The town of Shirley is where the property is located, and the Trustees land conservation group is the holder of this gem. An arboretum that was put together by former owner Arthur Banks in the 1960s is a highlight for those who like different trees. Many are not big yet, but the property holds some natural-grown Big Trees that add to the appeal. It was originally owned by Charles Goodspeed of Goodspeed Bookseller fame in Boston. Their vacation spot here was "Far" enough to take an effort to travel there but "Near" enough to visit often, so Far and Near was the given name. Arthur Banks was his grandson and started a "Pinetum" of special conifers as a part of the arboretum. The property also features a small golf course once used by locals and "Paradise," a hemlock-lined ravine that Spruce Swamp Brook runs through.

Ted Peterson and red oak.

Tortured beech.

When you arrive at the site, you park just past a small building in the parking area. Walk up the path beyond the kiosk and go through the gate. The sign will tell you to close the gate after you go through to prevent the deer from getting into the pinetum and nibbling up their hard work. Follow the path toward the covered picnic and restroom area and through some decent pine trees until you see the paper birch a short distance in. This attractive standout will draw your attention for a while, so take it in and enjoy. Birch is used for birch bark canoes, and in the spring the bark of branch-free trees can be peeled off in large sections and pieced together with sap for the canoe. Being such a short walk to it, you may want to continue on and then come back to spend a little more time there. Be sure to stay on the paths near the birch as there is a large planting of myrtle that has greened up around the tree and we don't want to damage it. Just past the birch is the start of the arboretum area, with some interesting trees beyond the covered fireplace. I happened upon Ted Peterson caring for the lawns and he gladly showed me some of the trees while I was there. Eli Rosina is the current manager of the property, who may be able to help if you have questions. Be sure to check out the tricolored beech, with leaves that turn three different colors.

Look for the tortured beech nearby and peek inside its draping canopy to see the tortured trunk of this unusual type of tree. Go behind it to find a grand specimen of red oak that takes up a large spot on the grounds. Ted said he worked here as a teenager and would sit under the tree with Arthur Banks and discuss important things like how much he would get paid for his work.

There is a bench nearby, so you could stop a while and discuss some important things in your life under the calming influence of this great tree. It was recently trimmed of dead and damaged branches in an attempt to keep it healthy. It's good to see some attempts to improve the health of old trees like this. I have seen many that have blown over at this stage in their life when their hollowing center and heavy branches make it difficult to stay standing. How much longer will we see this one survive? Thirty years? Fifty? I'm sure the trimming will help keep it around for some time.

A tool shed will draw you toward the conifers, and it would take some time to look around at them. They have ID tags for the most part and that will help with some of the unusual ones. I walked back toward the birch and took a hike on the trail over to Paradise Ravine and you may want to also. I was hoping for large hemlocks there but did not find any. It was likely cut over in the farming or sheep-raising era and has newer growth. I measured the height at about one hundred feet on a few, so still impressive, and the ravine is green and cooling on a hot summer day. Continue on along the Blue Trail near some wetland and past a large pine on your left that I did not measure, and around to a junction with a sign that brings you back through a gate to the Pinetum. Go up the hill and back where you started.

The birch sure is a standout and I hope you enjoy your time here as much as I did.

Difficulty Rating 1

Paper Birch

97" C   77' H   56' ACS   Total Points 188   Fair Condition
GPS: N 42.566897°   W 71.655694°
Δ State Champion

Red Oak

210" CBH   68' VH   74' ACS   Total Points 296   Fair Condition
GPS: N 42.566422°   W 71.656492°

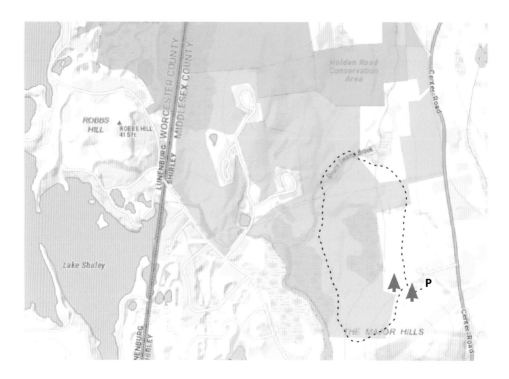

Directions

From Route 2, take Shirley Road, which changes to Lancaster Road at the town line. Go 2 miles to a right on Main Street and immediately bear left onto Center Road. Head north 1.7 miles to the entrance and parking area for the Far and Near Reservation on the left.

Wachusetts Meadows Wildlife Sanctuary

T his is one of the Massachusetts Audubon Society's gems for bird watching and walking the trails in the middle part of the state. There are trails laid out through the small hills, bordering wetlands and fields with great seating areas placed for the best views of wildlife and sunsets. One side seemed to have been open pasture with smaller trees now growing and one large white oak, while the other section had more mature trees scattered about along the trails. There is a visitor's center where you can get info about the property and the many events they put on. Stop in and say hi while dropping a reasonable $5 donation in the box near the rest rooms.

Start off by walking behind the center on the North Meadow Trail and catch the Birch Trail that goes around near the road and back to the Brown Hill Loop. Bearing left at the loop, be careful to stay on the trail, as I got onto an old trail with faded marks on the trees and luckily noticed the tree off to the left on the well-marked new trail. One way or another it will bring you to the main attraction for Big Tree enthusiast—the

Howling white oak.

white oak. It's in a great spot, with a bench to sit at while looking at the oak that may seem to be bored with your visit. The tree is highlighted on the map of the property and is being helped along with the girdling of the nearby pines so they won't grow tall, shading out the big and old but short oak.

White oak is better than the red oaks in many ways. It's stringier, with fibers that hold together and won't break as easily. It's used for steam-bent ribs in small boats and the main keels and stems in larger ones because it's more resistant to rot so holds up better in the water. I noticed the abundance of acorns from the red and black oaks along the trails, which was interesting because near me in New Hampshire we had hardly any acorns after having a great crop a year earlier. Seems like the heavy nut crops migrate around New England.

When moving on from the tree, you could continue on to catch the Summit Trail and either go up to the top or head back like I did to see the other side of the property. Once back at the parking area, I wandered around the sheep pasture past the open growing oak near the barn on the South Meadow Trail. Following near the wetland, you can look for some birds from an outlook with seats and then catch the Beaver Bend Trail. There are many pines maples and oaks here in the 2–3-foot-diameter range that must have grown in some time ago. Not old growth but newer growth that was managed to get to the prime size they are now for lumber. I was particularly impressed by a nice, straight sugar maple next to the trail. Keep on the trail and go left at the Pasture Trail, following it past a small pond and bearing left again to catch the Fern Forest Trail. This trail goes through a pine woods mixed with black cherry that seems to grow straighter here, offering a chance at a better harvest of cherry lumber than I see in NH, with the trees there somewhat stunted and crooked most of the time. Keep an eye out for one with a burl about 12' up. Burls are formed for different reasons such as an injury or stress at the site, but on cherry trees it is common for the growths to occur after a wasp lays eggs and a fungal or bacterial infection is introduced to the bark and the tree reacts by producing these strange growths.

It won't take you long to notice how the trail got its name. In October when I was here, the evergreen Christmas ferns were spreading all around with other ferns having died off from the cold; the trail must be thick with them all earlier in the year. At some point you will see something white in the distance on the ground and come up to the Quartz Boulder that is highlighted on the map.

Continue on to the Brook Trail and follow it to see the now-dead sugar maple that you would consider big for its type, especially in a woods setting. These dead snags are very important for the birds, mammals, insects, and fungus of the forest. I headed on to see the brook not far from the maple and noticed a few more, small, white-quartz stones. The Brook Loop continues across the brook, but I headed back the way I came, going left on the Fern Forest Trail to catch the Pasture Trail and then the Hemlock Seep Trail, that goes through a low wet seep with some of the few hemlocks I noticed on the property. I ended up West Trail and came to a gate with a good-sized ash and several oaks lining the road. With a great view up the road to the visitors center, I felt that although many of the trees on the Audubon land here are not of great size, there are a quite a few that are better than average and will draw your gaze. Those, along with the old-looking and Big Tree-sized yawning white oak and sugar maple, make it a worthwhile tour of these Central Massachusetts woods.

Difficulty Rating 2

White Oak

170" CBH   60' VH   57' ACS   Total Points 244   Fair Condition
GPS: N 42.458820° W 071.903721°

Dead Maple

162" CBH
GPS: N 42.458849° W 071.903725°

Directions

Get off I-90 onto Route 140 N in Sterling. Go 2.2 miles and take a left onto Route 62 W and go a bit over 4.5 miles to Goodnow Road on the right. Go about 1 mile to near the end, with the Wachusett Meadows Wildlife Sanctuary parking area on the right.

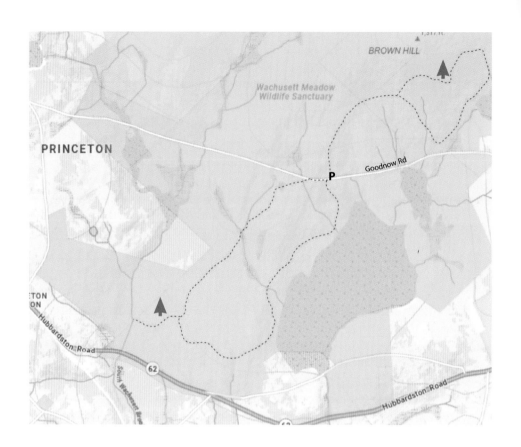

Smith College

This top-notch college campus was designed by Frederick Olmsted, who is famous for landscape designs at many estates, arboretums, and graveyards of the late 1800s. The trees here were planted around that time period and over the last 150 years or so have managed to reach great size for their type. The combination of continuous care with many arborists and botanists working here, and the Connecticut River Valley soils have enhanced their growth over that time period. The campus has an incredible conservatory with botanical gardens and a large greenhouse.

The college is right in the heart of Northampton, so there is lots to do, with many restaurants and shops. There are several bike and walking trails nearby. You could spend quite a bit of time here, so an overnight may be in order. Besides the trees I describe, there is a walking tour guide showing many of the Botanical Garden of Smith College plantings, which includes the whole 125-acre campus grounds. A map can be picked

Smith College entrance.

Plane tree and walker.

up at the Lyman Plant House and Conservatory. The map describes the trees and shows where they are.

There are five state champions here and a few more that I will highlight as significant in the state. The state champs are a ginkgo, London planetree, dawn redwood, tuliptree, and a Jersey elm. Others you may want to see include a camperdown elm, mountain silverbell, river birch, and black walnut. Use the Botanical Garden guide to find trees you like along the way. I should mention the American elms that are scattered all around on and off campus. They are injected on a regular basis to prevent Dutch elm disease, so it's a treat to see so many of them in a healthy state.

You can start the tour with the American elm near Campus Center in the greens. This is one of the over a dozen elms you can find here. At 184" C, it is larger than most I have seen. A bit short and without the classic elm vase shape but you can find that vase shape in others in town if you look around. The elms were a significant lumber source in the past and you can still get red or slippery elm at the retail hardwood suppliers. A good bending wood with interlocking grain, I have used both types in boat work over the years.

Ben checking ginkgo.

Head on over to the back side of the St John's Episcopal Church to see a very large black walnut. Its gray bark is camouflaged and interesting to see against the backdrop of the gray stone church. A gray squirrel was on it during my visit, adding to the color theme. The last few years were big years for oak acorns, with bumper crops everywhere and the result was a very large squirrel population in 2018. The walnuts here are an important food source with acorns on the decline this year. None are listed in the Mass tree list and both NH and VT have larger ones, but this is a very nice example of the species.

Wander over to Seelye lawn to get a look at the state champion London planetree. A cross between a sycamore and oriental planetree, it can grow to the great size of the sycamore, with this one and another nearby looking to keep growing, barring a major wind event. Very healthy examples set nicely in this square. The champion beats out any other northern New England tree of this type.

A burr oak is located on the other side of Seelye Hall, with its special mossy cup acorns giving it the alternate name of mossy cup oak. A neat-looking cap covers most of the acorn. You might be able to find some in the fall if the groundskeepers have not cleaned them up.

The dawn redwood to see is behind the Neilson Library. I could not get close during my visit as the building was being reconstructed in a way to save the outer shell, so at the time the walls were standing alone with support and no insides to the building. The outside was all fenced off for safety. It should be completed by now, so you can get closer to see the huge buttressed trunk. Pretty big for a tree that was thought to be extinct and planted in this country in the 1940s.

Make your way over to the greenhouse area from here to spend some time in the well-designed and relaxing garden area. Here you can see a ginkgo that rivals the largest I know of, in Montpelier, VT. It's a fitting tree for this garden area, as this ancient species is well-known in Asian cultures as a tree used to heal and improve brain function. Nearby is a Japanese umbrella pine with its neat-looking needles that cluster to form an umbrella shape, and beyond that a camperdown elm. For all those who desire a landscape-improving tree, this is a must-have with its small stature and drooping branches. It brings your eyes down from the larger trees to your garden in a very appealing way. This particular tree was grafted with another type of elm to enhance the effect. It's not listed as a champion but is good-sized and hard to take your eyes off of. The leaves seem to shimmer in the light and stand out when looking from certain angles.

You may want to explore other plants while in the conservatory area. For a small donation, you can look through the plant house and conservatory with many flowers, ferns, cactus, and ivy. Brochures describe the edible and medicinal plants on hand and what you will see in the outdoor gardens surrounding the greenhouse.

To continue on with the trees, go out on College Lane toward Elm Street. A bench overlooking Paradise Pond is against a pretty nice sycamore. Look for the single fruit or seed balls that differentiate it from the London planetree, which has two per stem. Down in the lawn, you can't miss the columnar English oak with its narrow crown and unique look.

Take a left at the stop before you get to Elm Street and go to the President's House with its magnificent mountain silverbell. The bark gives it an appeal on its own, but in the spring it is most impressive with the whole tree awash with showy white flowers. I like the look of the root system showing on the hillside next to the house. While looking around here, you can check out the gardens around the house, then wander toward Paradise Pond and look for the Japanese meditation garden and the nearby wildflower and woodlands garden trail.

Tuliptree in woodlot.

Viewing all these trees and other plants will take a good part of your day, but to finish things off be sure to allow some time to head over to Columbus Avenue to look at the state champion pin oak and the tuliptree in the woods off Lyman Road. Look at the oak from sidewalk or road and be sure to respect the private property of the house next to it. Then head to the preschool parking lot off Lyman Road. A trail goes into the woods near the sidewalk for the preschool. Head down the trail and start looking around at the several large tuliptrees that greet you. The most impressive thing is their height; the one with biggest circumference I measured is 133' tall. These tuliptrees are called tulip or yellow poplar, even though they are in the magnolia family, but their lumber is mixed in at the retail suppliers as poplar. It's soft for a hardwood, known for

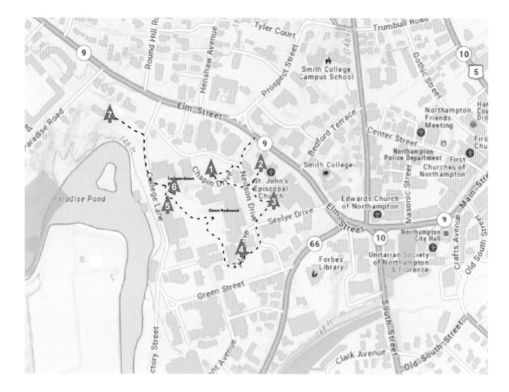

its stability and simple appearance, so it's used for upholstered furniture frames and backup plywood for more decorative woods. The trees Latin name means lily tree because of its tulip-like flowers.

Difficulty Rating 1 to 2   For distance and time to see them all.

1. American Elm

184" CBH   73.5' VH   91' ACS   Total Points 280   Good Condition
GPS: N 42.318817°   W 72.638592°

2. Black Walnut

150" CBH   76' VH   83.5' ACS   Total Points 247   Excellent Condition
GPS: N 42.318981°   W 72.637163°

3. London Planetree

185" CBH   103' VH   106' ACS   Total Points 314   Excellent Condition
GPS: N 42.318291°   W 72.637002°
Δ State Champion

4. Burr Oak

148" CBH
GPS: N 42.317437° W 72.637368°

5. Ginkgo

206' CBH   81.5' VH   70' ACS   Total Points 305   Excellent Condition
GPS: N 42.318363° W 72.639854°
Δ **State Champion**

6. Japanese Umbrella Pine

99.6' CBH   45.5' VH   31' ACS   Total Points 152.8   Good Condition
GPS: N 42.318452° W 72.639804°
Δ **State Champion**

7. Mountain Silverbell

90.6" CBH   67' VH   51' ACS   Total Points 170   Excellent Condition
GPS: N 42.319976° W 72.641598°

8. Pin Oak *(not shown on map)*

222" CBH   111' VH   106' ACS   Total Points 359   Good Condition
GPS: N 42. 310925° W 72.633561°
Δ **State Champion**

9. Tuliptree *(not shown on map)*

171" CBH   137' VH   74' ACS   Total Points 326   Good Condition
GPS: N 42.313187° W 72.631018°

Directions

From I-91, take Route 5 to the center of Northampton. Park at the parking garage on Armory Street or find another spot around town. I think the meters have a two-hour limit, so the garage may be better. Walk through town to get a feel for the area and keep an eye out for an eatery that you will need to visit after your tree tour. Go along Main Street to Elm Street/Route 9 and go into the campus on Neilson Drive, or to get to the Lyman Conservatory, keep going to College Lane and follow that down to the waterfront and the plant house area.

Trees 8 and 9 are not shown on the map but can be visited by following the directions in the description on page 111.

Bidwell House Champion Oak

The small town of Monterey was established as Township #1 in 1737 with the Rev. Adonijah Bidwell as its first minister. The home stayed in the family until 1853. In the early 1900s, the Berkshire Summer School of Arts was founded here and attracted students who were housed in forty-five cabins on the property next door, which stayed in use until 1936. The house was sold off to private owners in 1926. From the 1960s to the 1980s, the owners replicated the interior of the house to the 1770s time period. They managed to buy the original estate inventory from the 1700s and used it as a guide for the restoration work. In 1990, it was turned over to the public as a museum.

The museum grounds now include an interpretive trail with info on the Mohican Tribe that used this area for their hunting grounds. The large red oak on the property may not have been here when the Native Americans roamed the grounds, but was here for many of the occupants after that time period.

The grounds are open to the public at no charge. You can park in the parking area and head up to the house and to the right toward the hunting camp and herb garden, where the trail starts on the far-left side of the fence. Head out on the Turkeybush Trail, down past the Poets Tree, and continue about a ½ mile to a cairn of rocks on the left with a handwritten sign for the Champion Oak Trail. Follow that past some other oaks that you may think are large enough but keep going until the trail ends at the biggest. It may have been a champion oak at one time, but there are other oaks measured in the state as somewhat larger than this. I think you will find that it's large enough, with a 4½-foot diameter making it worthy of your trip to this out-of-the-way town.

A bonus black cherry tree that you passed on your way in is at the side of the lane between the parking area and the house, near the red shed. It seemed to be in pretty good condition, although a bit hidden with some vines climbing the trunk when I visited. Someone probably should nominate it as a legacy or champion tree.

All-in-all, a great spot to get some history of early life in this part of the state while getting in a decent walk to some Big Trees.

Bidwell House former champion oak.

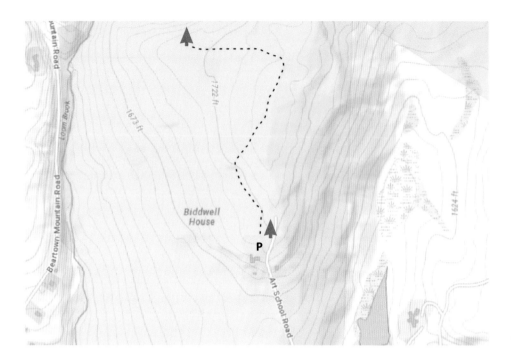

Difficulty Rating 1

Red Oak

168" CBH   75' VH   81' ACS   Total Points 270   Fair Condition
GPS: N 42.21186°   W 73.22077°

Black Cherry

140" CBH   91' VH   63' ACS   Total Points 247   Good Condition
GPS: N 42.208093°   W 73.218394°
Δ Possible State Champion

Directions

From Route 23/Maine Road in Monterey Village, go north 1.5 miles on
Tyringham Road to Art School Road, then go left 1mile, and then follow
signs to the parking lot for the museum.

A fee is charged for entrance to the museum. Grounds are open free
of charge.

Tanglewood

The well-known music venue for the Berkshires also holds some of the largest trees in the area. The state champion Norway spruce is found near a back entrance and one of the state's largest paper birches is on the lawn of the Tappan Manor House Visitors Center. I found the state-listed black locust to be multi-trunk trees and did not measure them, but I did find a few worthwhile pines at 140" CBH and 153" CBH that should be fully measured. I ran out of time, so only got the height of the smaller one at 119'. The grounds are well-kept, and the trees here are lucky enough to be fed, pruned if needed, and pampered all year long.

In the early 1930s, the New York Philharmonic and the Boston Symphony Orchestra performed well-attended concerts in the Berkshires. In 1936, the Tappan Family Estate was offered as a gift to the Boston Symphony Orchestra so they could keep performing in the area, and

Double-trunked paper birch.

State champion Norway spruce.

thus Tanglewood was born. In 1986, the neighboring Highwood Estate was acquired, greatly expanding the grounds. Tanglewood is now the summer home of the Boston Symphony Orchestra and its Academy, the Boston Pops, and the Tanglewood Music Center. They provide training for all types of musicians and concert venues of all types throughout the summer. Be sure to check out their performance schedule before your visit.

Start your tree tour here with the white oak in the center lawn by the main stage. This is seen in many photos of Tanglewood and I'm sure its shade is enjoyed by concert goers while attending a show here. A few grounding cables to prevent lightning strikes have been added. I did not see signs of strikes, so it looked pretty healthy. Not real big at 152" C, its open growth made it spread out instead of growing high, so it's only 58' tall. Can't beat its home turf though. Next, head over toward the Tappan Manor House, and in the side yard you will notice several white or paper birch trees. The largest is double-trunked, but one of the trunks still measures close to the state champ and likely ties it. These birches add quite an appeal to the landscaping around the house.

The Norway spruce is not far away, if going back toward the center stage just beyond the house to the right, near the sidewalk to a back entrance gate. The state champion has quite the circumference and is among a line of these appealing landscape trees. This weeping branch type of spruce is seen planted around many estates old and new.

I was told the locust trees are way down beyond the main stage and past some other buildings, so I headed over to check them out. I didn't measure them but found some very nice white pines near a building and a fenced in area at the very left of the site. These are standouts for the area, and, while not real tall, they have good circumferences.

We had often heard of music events at Tanglewood but were never able to attend one. My wife could not resist the urge to carry and play her ukulele while on the grounds. If you love music and Big Trees, this outstanding regional attraction is the place to visit.

Difficulty Rating 1

1. White Oak

152" CBH   58' VH   97' ACS   Total Points 234   Good Condition
GPS: N 42.34915°   W 073.31103°

2. Paper Birch

96" CBH   78' VH   55' ACS   Total Points 187   Good Condition
GPS: N 42.34921°   W 073.31284°
Δ State Champion

3. Norway Spruce

165" CBH   109' VH   48' ACS   Total Points 286   Good Condition
GPS: N 42.34858°   W 073. 31142°
Listed as 176" CBH in 2010
Δ State Champion

4 & 5. White Pines (2)

1st pine: 140" CBH   119' VH
2nd pine: 153" CBH   Needs measuring   Good Condition
GPS: N 42.34851°   W 073.30818°   Close to each other.

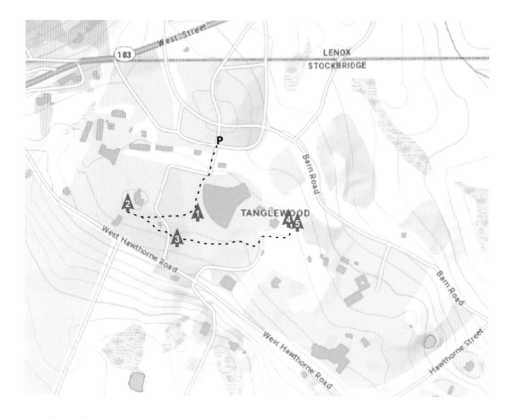

Directions

From Main Street in Stockbridge, take Church Street or Route 102 just under 1½ miles and turn right onto Interlaken Road or 183. Follow it just over 4 miles to the entrance of Tanglewood on the right.

From Interstate 90, get off on Route 20 N and go through the town of Lee, continuing about 4 miles to Route 183 W. Go 2.5 miles to the entrance for Tanglewood on the left.

Note that the grounds are open 9 a.m. to 3 p.m. free of charge, except on performance days when they have music playing. They clear the grounds before the gates open for the performance. You must purchase a ticket to enter for those concert times.

Cobble Cottonwood

In the town of Sheffield, on the western end of Massachusetts near the Connecticut border, is a Trustees property called Bartholomew's Cobble, declared as a National Natural Landmark because of the many different plant types found here. The combination of soil type and its location at the northern and southern limits for many species makes it a special place where these species co-exist. The property borders the Huscatonic River, supplying the water for the many farms in the area and also a for very large cottonwood. This is one of the largest trees you will see in the state.

Park at the parking area and start along the Ledges Trail past the not-so-high ledges that hover over you. This is the front of the "cobble," which is from the German word for a small rocky hill. If you want to see some small caves and check out the top of the cobble, take the Ledges Trail around the other side of the cobble and the Craggy Knoll Trail over the top. To continue to the tree, go past the tractor path to the junction with Bailey Trail and take that along the river and past a neat elm, big pine, and a few large cottonwoods you will see on the left. Keep going past the junction with Tulip Tree Trail along the edge of the floodplain until you come to the tallest and second-largest-overall cottonwood listed in the state.

I love the deeply fissured bark and brownish-red color on these large cottonwoods. A main branch has fallen and the center is hollow, so it's not in the best shape but is holding out fairly well. It is said that several people have climbed into that small hole in the trunk side at once. When settlers were moving westward in this country, they kept a lookout for cottonwood groves because they always grew near water. Sometimes a lone traveler would move into these large trees for brief periods. Occasionally, they would become a more permanent home for those who did not have the means to build a homestead. It must have been concerning when the wind swayed their homes back and forth.

The wood is lightweight, colorless, tasteless, and has no odor, making it ideal for its primary use as fruit boxes and crates. It is somewhat soft and can be easily carved, so it can be used as a substitute for basswood or linden when carving. The Hopi and Pueblo tribes carve their kachina

Some of our largest trees are cottonwoods.

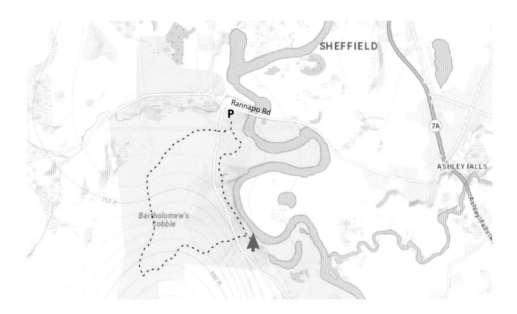

dolls from cottonwood roots because that is where the good spirits lived.

We went back via the Tulip Tree Trail and up to the open fields of Herbert's Hill to take in the scenic vista of the nearby hills, then back along the tractor path to where we started. I wish I had checked out the cobble better, so you may want to go back that way or check it out on your way to the cottonwood. The tuliptree is medium-sized and has quite a bit of undergrowth around it. I had hoped that it was a natural-growing example, as it is close to its natural southern growing range, but it is likely an escapee from a nearby planting.

Difficulty Rating 2   For round trip.

237" CBH   116' VH   72' ACS   Total Points 371   Poor Condition
GPS: N 42.05124° W 073.34796°

Directions

Bear right onto 7A or Ashley Falls Road, go ½ mile to a right onto Rannapo Road, and continue 1.5 miles to a curve and take the right onto Weatogue Road to Bartholomew's Cobble Nature Center and the trail starting point.

30 *Stockbridge, Cummington, Williamsburg, Carlisle, Concord*

Eastern White Pines [*Pinus strobus*]

Massachusetts has white pines that are taller than those in the more northerly states in New England. The soil is better in some areas and the climate is moderate, allowing more growing time. The tallest are in and around the Berkshire Mountains, and a long weekend spent in that area would allow you to see most of them in this part of the state. I visited some of the largest I had heard of, but others can be found along Route 2 in the Mohawk Trail State Forest and Dunbar Brook if you want to search them out.

The tours here include the Ice Glen in Stockbridge, the William Cullen Bryant Homestead in Cummington, Mass Audubon's Graves Farm Wildlife Sanctuary in Williamsburg, the Carlisle Pines in Lincoln, and The Old Rifle Range in Concord. Most of these are old pine forests with many large trees besides the ones highlighted. A few other types, like hemlock and especially the cherry at the Bryant Homestead, will be seen too. Pines not noted here are included in some of the other tree tours.

The Ice Glen

The Berkshires are excellent for a few days of Big Tree hunting. One of the biggest pines in Massachusetts is within walking distance of the center of town. A trail starting at the end of Park Street goes through a stone gate, then across the Housatonic River on a suspended bridge. After you cross the RR tracks, keep bearing right and up when coming to junctions as the trail is not marked well. This brings you in between two ridges and through a jumble of rocks in what is called the Ice Glen. It's protected from the sun and summer heat by the many old and large trees, with the rocks holding the icy frosts of winter well into the summer. The Laurel Hill Association and town of Stockbridge does an impressive job of maintaining the trail by cutting the huge logs that fall across it and keeping the many rock steps that aid you while scrambling in good working condition

The large trees are all near the trail for the most part, and hemlocks and pines over 10 feet in circumference and 120 feet tall are common. The boulders and ledges are another draw that deserve some exploring. They are covered with moss and ferns, giving a very impressive look in some areas. The trail goes over and through large boulders, many times they are hanging over your heads. Look for those with small caves under them that I am sure harbor some wild creatures in the protected dark corners.

Your scrambling efforts are soon rewarded. Where a house nearby marks the end of the trail, you will be next to the largest pine and hemlock on the property. There are very few pines of this size in northern New England. Hemlocks of this height are not that common either. After some time with these natural wonders, head back the way you came. The path seems much quicker and easier going in the other direction. After your hike, be sure to go into town for lunch at one of the restaurants. Stockbridge still harbors Alice's Restaurant that Arlo Guthrie made famous with the song of the same name, albeit with different owners. It was not open the day we went, so we ate a great lunch at Once Upon a Table, which is down a side alley with many shops surrounding it.

Difficulty Rating 2

Eastern White Pine

160" CBH   145' VH   46' ACS   Total Points 316.5   Good Condition
GPS: N 42.27197°   W 073.30775°

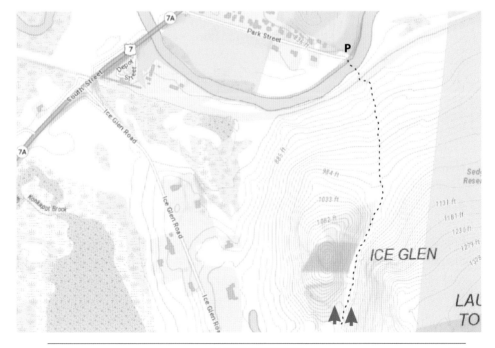

Eastern Hemlock

131.5" CBH   128' VH   39' ACS   Total Points 269.5   Good Condition
GPS: Same as pine above, just across trail.

William Cullen Bryant Homestead

William Cullen Bryant spent his childhood at this home on the foothills of the Berkshires and then went on to become a famous poet and editor of the *New York Evening Post* in the mid-1800s. His editorials helped get funding or support for things like creating Frederick Law Olmsted's Central Park in New York City and Abraham Lincoln's bid for president. The rural features in the area gave him inspiration for some of his poems. It became his summer home later in life. You can appreciate some of the natural features in the same way as he did by hiking around the Trivulet and Big Pines trails on the land he purchased across the street in order to preserve the forest there.

You could start at the house and pay the fee to see the home set up the way it was after he renovated it into the Victorian cottage you see now. It is filled with three generations of furnishings and exotic items from Bryant's travels in Europe and Asia. From the house cross the field, following the Rivulet Trail and cross the street past the kiosk to wander into the woods along the rivulet. This is a small ravine with a stream flowing through the bottom. The trail follows the top edge, and there are signs with a few of the poems inspired here for you to wonder about. The trees seen include some old-looking hemlocks and hardwoods like cherry, ash, maple, and birch. One is an outstandingly large cherry tree. Probably the best I have seen in my travels preparing this book. While there are some larger, they are not of the quality of this with its long, winding, clear trunk.

Continue on to the far end of the Rivulet Trail turning into the woods. When you come to its junction with the Pine Loop Trail, take the Pine Loop and you will immediately be confronted with a huge pine next to the trail. These are tall trees for the most part, and this one and several others have been measured for decades. The early measurements had them taller and, as is common for many of this species, the wind has taken the tops off and the uppermost spires of branches are now the highest point, at 10' or 15' smaller. If you have a clinometer and want to measure others with the tops still there, I think you will find a few at 160', which are among the tallest in the region.

Going on from this first tree, you eventually come to a spot where the trails winds through several that are bunched together, making for an impressive scene of large old-growth trees not seen in too many forests nowadays. Many are in the 11' to 12' circumference range and 130' to 150' tall. The largest in circumference is at the far western edge of the property, and you have to go off the trail and cross a small ravine to see it. The bark is deeper and coarser on this giant, but with its side rotted on the front and a large crack starting in the back, it likely will be blown over soon in a strong windstorm. There are many of those blow-downs littering the woods here, making travel a bit more difficult. Continuing on the Pine Trail, you pass several more good-sized pines and come to the junctions of the Rivulet Trail as it loops around. Follow it a little further and it connects back near the Rivulet and out to the road. All in all, an outstanding forest to visit any time of year. Be sure to stop at the Old Creamery Coop for refreshments when back on the road.

Difficulty Rating 2

1. Cherry

111" CBH   98' VH   40' ACS   Total Points 219   Good Condition
GPS: N 42.470619°   W 072.927847°
Δ State Champion

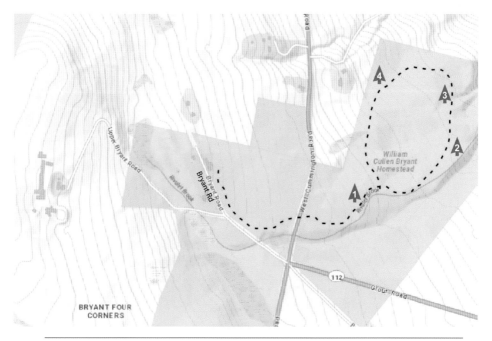

2. Pine #1

139" CBH   147' VH   43' ACS   Total Points 296   Excellent Condition
GPS: N 42.472706°   W 072.927122°

3. Pine #2

139" CBH   143' VH   39' ACS   Total Points 292   Good Condition
GPS: N 42.473448°   W 072.927629°

4. Biggest Circumference Pine

158" CBH   141' VH   33' ACS   Total Points 307   Poor Condition
GPS: N 42.474393°   W 072.927968°

Directions

Heading west on Route 112 from Cummington, turn left at the Old Creamery Coop where 112 forks off from Route 9. Continue for 1½ miles to the fifth corner and go straight on Bryant Road to the homestead.

Graves Farm Wildlife Sanctuary

This is a trail to an eastern white pine that is worth taking if you are in the Smith College area looking at trees. The Graves family of dairy farmers were also avid birders and kept records of what they saw here. To preserve the 700 acres for wildlife, they decided to donate it to the

Graves pine.

Massachusetts Audubon Society, which now manages it with that purpose in mind. The group has more than 130,000 members and cares for 36,000 acres of conserved land in Mass. Much of this land is open to the public to encourage you to see and appreciate the wildlife in the state, so feel free to join them or donate a few dollars at the donation boxes that they keep on some lands.

Several brooks run through the Graves property and drain into the Mill River. Nonnie Day Brook can be seen at the end of the loop where you will find the pine that we are looking for. This Big Tree along with many others has an important connection to a water source. The Nonnie Day fills this tree's watering needs, allowing it to reach the great size seen here. The nearby marsh is also a source of water, so it keeps growing and growing. You will find this water connection with many of the giants seen in your Big Tree searches.

When first entering the trail, it may be hard to find your way but just keep a look-out for the round, blue and yellow markers on the trees and you will stay on the trail just fine. The woods are cool and shady, with many pines that will eventually get bigger. If you go left around the loop trail to the brook, you end up near the marsh where the loop turns back, and if you look a little, the impressive Graves Pine will show itself. With

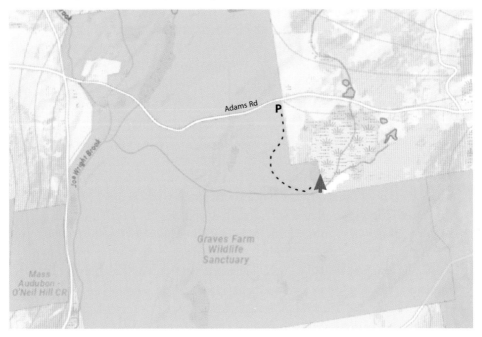

a circumference of just under 12', it is not the largest but is big enough to impress and quite tall. Not just the pine but other trees, the brook, marsh, and undergrowth of swamp azaleas make it a nice spot to hang around a while. While crossing the brook on a log to get the trees height measurement, I was greeted by several small sparrows who did not seem to mind my visit. It's a rather short walk to the tree and if more exercise is in order continue on the Graves Brothers Loop Trail.

Difficulty Rating 1

141" CBH   133' VH   54' ACS   Total Points 287   Good Condition
GPS: N 42.39868°   W 072.70040°

Directions

From Route 9 in Williamsburg, take Depot Road to an intersection. Go right on Adams Road and go 0.6 miles and up a hill to the parking area on the right. There is no parking on the road and keep in mind that the lot is not plowed in the winter.

Carlisle Pines

The Carlisle Pines are well-known in this part of Massachusetts. The forest was saved from logging in 1901 and turned over to the AMC as a public reserve. There were over one hundred mature trees at that time, but the hurricane of 1938 came through and most of them were lost to the winds. Now there are about a dozen pines and hemlocks of considerable size, making it a worthwhile walk through some woods that are very close to the urban center of Boston. This will give you an idea of what the forests of old must have been like. Imagine walking through here if the hurricane had not passed through. The land is now controlled by the state through nearby Great Brook Farm State Park.

These pines have a unique look to their bark. Instead of the deep, chunky texture of many of the old-growth eastern white pines, the bark has wider and longer plated sections that you might see in something like a red pine with thinner bark. Maybe it's because the trees grew fast just as the bark was maturing when the woods were opened up from the hurricane. Some have said it could be just the genetics of these particular trees.

A trail starts at the end of Forest Park Drive. As you walk through, keep left at the junction and go down near a wet area where you will start

Measuring Carlisle pine.

seeing the trees. We measured the largest hemlock right on the trail. It is comparable to the Codman North hemlock in circumference but a little taller. Further along the trail, as you make a turn to go up the hill, is the most impressive pine. Close to 11' in circumference, it is among the largest you will see in this part of the state. You get a little feel for

the old woods while here. If you want to keep that feeling a bit longer, then go back the way you came or you can finish your walk through the seeming miniature pines that are on the uplands part of the return loop.

Difficulty Rating 2

Pine

131" CBH   118.5' VH   38.5' ACS   Total Points 259   Good Condition
GPS: N 42.54429° W 071.38261°

Hemlock

138" CBH   111.5' VH   38' ACS   Total Points 259   Good Condition
GPS: N 42.54391° W 071.38325°

Directions

From Route 225 in Carlisle, take Curve Street go about 0.4 miles and bear left onto Forest Park Road. At 0.16 miles, bear right, staying on Forest Park Drive where it meets Evergreen Lane. Go to the end and park off the road as much as you can. The trail starts right ahead of you.

Old Rifle Range

Concord seems to be the spot to see some very big and tall pines. It must be the confluence of the rivers here and the Thoreau and Emerson history in the town that inspired the early conservation of land. This particular property was set aside by the town as a rifle range in 1910 to train the Massachusetts Volunteer Militia and was used until soldiers were deployed for WWI. It was kept in use until turned over to the Town Forest and Rec Commission in 1958. The remnants of the target berms and target raising mechanisms can still be seen along the main trail that leads along the edge of Ministerial Swamp to Kennedy's Pond.

It's a good hour walk to the pond and back, and you are bound to see some birds and other wildlife along the way. There are many older pines of fair size spread on the northern side of the property. After getting away from the swamp and passing the last target berm, the first big pine you come to is at a trail junction and can't be missed, with a large circumference and a double trunk forking at about 15' up. It must have been more open-grown because there are a number of large dead branches going up the tree.

I was more impressed with the second big pine, which is north or

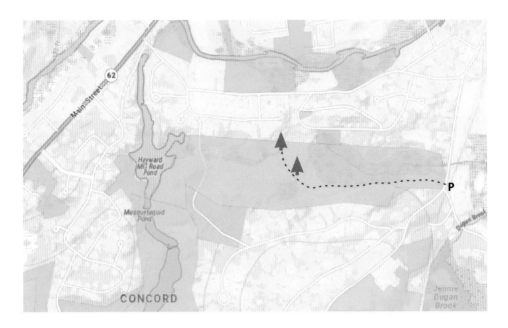

right off the yellow trail onto the red trail. After crossing the wet area and going up toward some houses, keep an eye open on the left for some larger pines and pick out the biggest. Go into the woods a little to the tree and the shape and form will show why I like it better. There are not many pines of this stature in the northeastern part of Massachusetts and Concord seems to have managed to keep some around.

Difficulty Rating 2

Biggest Pine

152" CBH   122' VH   46' ACS   Total Points 285   Good Condition
GPS: N 42.445008°   W 071.404571°

2nd Pine

135" CBH   120' VH   47.5' ACS   Total Points 267   Excellent Condition
GPS: N 42.445969°   W 071.404442°

Directions

Take Route 62 west about 2 miles out of the center of Concord. Go left onto Cottage Street, which changes to Old Marlboro Road. Follow it just under 1 mile to the parking area for the Old Rifle Range on the right.

New Hampshire

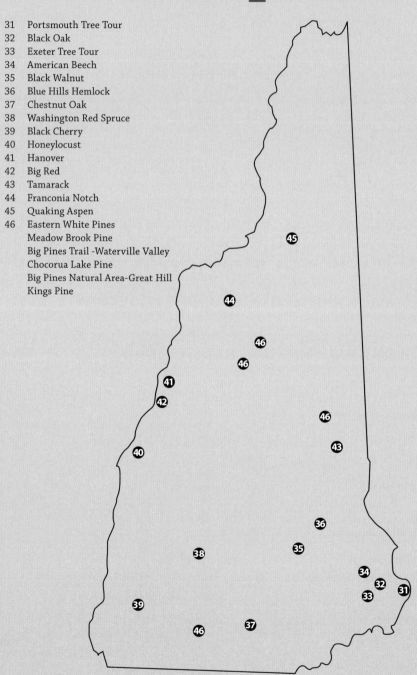

31 Portsmouth Tree Tour
32 Black Oak
33 Exeter Tree Tour
34 American Beech
35 Black Walnut
36 Blue Hills Hemlock
37 Chestnut Oak
38 Washington Red Spruce
39 Black Cherry
40 Honeylocust
41 Hanover
42 Big Red
43 Tamarack
44 Franconia Notch
45 Quaking Aspen
46 Eastern White Pines
    Meadow Brook Pine
    Big Pines Trail -Waterville Valley
    Chocorua Lake Pine
    Big Pines Natural Area-Great Hill
    Kings Pine

"Entering Portsmouth as the Moon Rises"
1995, Reduction Woodcut, edition 25, size 22 x 32 in., by Don Gorvett;
Photo Credit: George Barker.

Portsmouth Big Tree Tour

I am a native of Portsmouth and love this town, and I'm sure you will too. The small city has a long history as a seacoast port and some of the trees have been around since the American Revolution. There are quite a few European beech trees spread throughout that grow to a great girth and were planted as ornamentals in front of the architecturally interesting buildings here. This tour will take you to some of these historically significant homes, to a quiet park by a mill pond, near the town offices, and to the South Cemetery. This is a good town for bike riding, so you can bring your bikes or take the time for a leisurely walk, absorbing much that the downtown has to offer. There is so much to do here that you will likely have to come back a few times to get the feel of things. There are many top-notch restaurants and simpler sandwich shops when you get hungry. A rest stop can be made at Prescott Park on the mighty Piscataqua River overlooking the Portsmouth Naval Shipyard. I have spent many a day here eating a Moe's Italian Sandwich and enjoying the scenery. The historic homes offer tours which can be fascinating if you want to know about the people that lived there and their connection to New Hampshire and our country.

You can take a ride on the new gundalow that is a replica of the old sailing barges that were used to transport goods up and down the river. There is also a tour boat, the *Thomas Leighton*, that will bring you seven miles out to sea to the Isles of Shoals. That should keep you busy, but let's get back to the trees.

To start your visit, you can park at the parking area near the corner of Pleasant Street and Junkins Avenue, or if too full, try the parking garage in the center of town off Hanover Street. Make your way to the Langdon House at 143 Pleasant Street to get started viewing the trees. The white house with a white fence has a European beech in the yard next to the house. It's a double trunked tree but will give you a feel of how big this type of tree can get. There were two others in town that were state champs and quite a bit larger, but both were recently taken down. The grounds are open to the public and you should be able to walk through the gate by the driveway. If not, ask to see the trees at the building

Jerry Langdon at the Langdon House with Douglas fir.

that leads the tours. If you allow enough time, you may also consider paying the fee to take a tour of the house. While on the grounds, be sure to go out back through the arbor to the softwood plantings out back. The county champion Douglas fir is there along with some impressive Norway spruce. When ready, head toward downtown and up past the North Church. Keep going straight onto Market Street or, because this is a one-way road, if on bikes you will have to go right on State Street, just past the Langdon House and around to Bow Street, then to Market Street. You will enjoy the trip either way.

Once on Market Street, go down a few blocks to 154 Market Street and you will see the Moffett Ladd House and its horse chestnut tree beside it. This is the largest of this type in the state, and it is no wonder due to its history. This tree, which is on the National Register of Historic trees, was planted by General William Whipple in 1776 to celebrate his signing of the Declaration of Independence. One day, I watched an arborist show his climbing skills and how he sets up the cables that help keep the large limbs from breaking off. You can see the tree from the sidewalk or take a tour of the house and view it up close. After, you could take a side trip through the garden area across the street into Ceres Street with its restaurants and storefronts, then view the tugboats that work on the river and dock here. Make your way back into the center of town and go down Congress Street to the intersection with Middle Street. Cross at the crosswalk to the Discovery Center. You could visit

Red maple.

there to learn more about the town and see some of the local art on exhibit. On the Islington Street side of the Discovery Center, take a look at the European linden in the side yard. These are similar to our native basswood but with smaller leaves. Both types are known for their soft lumber, which is sought after by wood carvers because it is easy to work and will not crack or check. Continue back onto Middle Street and across State Street then onto Route 1. You can take a side trip at the second right to Austin Street, go two houses down and take a look from the sidewalk at the European beech inside the fence. There is another at the other end of the yard.

Go back to Route 1 to a left at the lights on Miller Avenue, also known as Route 1A. Continue on to the intersection with Rockland Street, then go left on Rockland and right on Richards Avenue to get away from the busier Route 1A traffic. Go to the end and cross South Street to the South Cemetery. In the cemetery, you will find a European larch on the South Street end. These trees were planted in the northeastern part of the US and Canada and have become naturalized to the US. This means they are recognized by American Forests as a tree that can reproduce naturally in areas where they are planted, and are treated the same as a native tree in the Big Tree Program. This species is similar to our native tamarack, but the cones are a bit larger on the European version. This tree has some discoloration on the side, probably from a wound up higher on the side causing the sap to drip down the tree. There are a few others in the cemetery that are worth seeing in their fall colors. This type is one of the few softwoods that have needles which turn golden yellow, then fall off for the winter. Some homes have these or tamaracks planted in the yard as ornamentals and then the home sells and the new owner cuts the tree down thinking that it has died because the needles fell off. If you see these in November, their golden needles will be at their best. Get back on the main cemetery road to the left or east and walk along until you come to the one-time state champion red maple that is now second largest in the state. This species seems to grow at times with a twist like you see in this trunk. In the spring, the road will be covered with the red flower petals that help ID this tree. Where I live on the river, they are abundant and a sure sign of spring is when I see the petals floating down the river.

Be sure to check out some of the Norway spruces at the far end of the cemetery near Route 1A, then walk or ride back to South Street. Go right into Clough Park right next door and inside the fence you will see a crack willow. It does not have the familiar drooping branches of the weeping willow we all know, but is closely related. Even though this is good-sized and the county champion, they can get quite a bit larger. Continue down the road to a left at Junkins Avenue and you will see the parking lot for the city offices on the right. This was the old hospital, and in between the parking lots is a large catalpa that is worth checking out. They have large leaves and long seedpods that hang off the branches all year long. I was not familiar with this tree as I do not see them in the woods near me but remember seeing the seed pods on the sidewalks as a child living in town. Head down Junkins Avenue, past the mill ponds and take a right on a small side road into Haven Park near the start of this tour. This is a small park, with green grass growing under a full canopy of good-sized oaks. They must provide plenty of acorns to feed the huge gray squirrels that live here. You will also see an American beech down near the South Mill Pond overlooking the old hospital. With so many large trees in one area, it is impressive to see them and they give you a forest feel in the center of town. Hang around a while to get the feel of the park, look at the statue of Civil War General Fitz John Porter and try out the benches.

Relax and think back on your tour of the trees in this impressive port city of Portsmouth.

Difficulty 2 Traffic.

1. Douglas Fir

90" CBH   103' VH   28' ACS   Total Points 200   Good Condition
GPS: N 43.075700° W 070.754917°
Δ State Champion

2. Horse Chestnut

204" CBH   66' VH   78' ACS   Total Points 290   Good Condition
GPS: N 43.078816° W 070.758315°
Δ State Champion

3. European Linden

129" CBH   74' VH   42' ACS   Total Points 213   Good Condition
GPS: N 43.075517° W 070.761145°

4. European Larch

103" CBH   89' VH   37' ACS   Total Points 204   Good Condition
GPS: N 43.065664° W 070.756709°

5. Red Maple

162" CBH   66' VH   53' ACS   Total Points 241   Good Condition
GPS: N 43.064729° W 070.755278°
Δ Former State Co-Champion

6. Norway Spruce

155" CBH   72' VH   40' ACS   Total Points 237   Good Condition
GPS: N 43.062217° W 070.754717°

7. Crack Willow

187" CBH   51' VH   41' ACS   Total Points 248   Poor Condition
GPS: N 43.067233° W 070.756233°
Δ State Champion

8. Catalpa

148" CBH   59' VH   53' ACS   Total Points 221   Poor Condition
GPS N 43.070217° W 070.754283°

9. Haven Park Oak

183" CBH   75' VH   64' ACS   Total Points 274   Excellent Condition
GPS: N 43.074133°   W 070.754300°

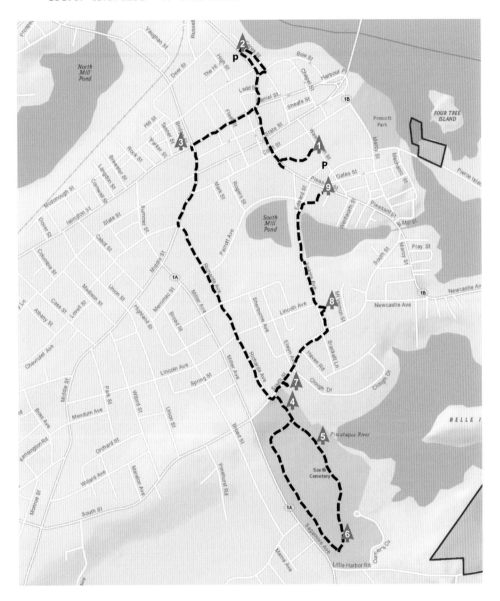

Black Oak *[Quercus velutina Lam.]*

The Great Bay Discovery Center in Greenland is a hub for activity across this significant natural resource of coastal New Hampshire. Great Bay is recognized as a National Estuarine Research Reserve and this property serves as the educational headquarters. Inside the center, there are educational exhibits, including a touch tank so the kids can look at and pick up some of the creatures that live in the brackish water here. The water of three rivers meets in the bay, with four other rivers joining in as they all drain out with the tides, creating one of the swiftest tidal currents in the nation as it goes down the Piscataqua River past Portsmouth and out to the ocean. There are many activities at the center, including educational programs and kayak trips on the water. You could plan a summer day here and take a side trip to the black oak. There

Myleigh and black oak.

Red oak vs. black oak buds.

are a few easy trails that go down across a boardwalk over the marsh and to a lookout across Great Bay. The Wigwam Trail goes in away from the waterfront past a birchbark wigwam and to this wide-bottomed black oak that sits near the RR tracks. Its chunky bark gives it away as a black and not red oak. Some I have seen are less telling with the bark, so you may have to use several key features to ID a black oak. In the fall when the leaves are down, you can pick up some of the small twigs that have buds attached and look them over. The black has larger fuzzy tan buds compared to the smaller reddish and shinier red oak buds. The black oak twigs have a coarser feel with white spots or hairs on them, while the red oak twigs are smoother and shiny. Another way to tell is by the mature acorns which are larger on the red oak, which has a cap that sits on top like a summer hat. The smaller black oak acorn has a winter hat cap pulled further down over about ½ the acorn. At times, acorns can take on different characteristics that can make red oak acorns look like black oak acorns and vice versa, so try to find several acorns to compare along with bud and leaf inspections for proper ID.

Start out from the center and take the main trail to the boardwalk. Any children with you will enjoy seeing the painted animal tracks that cross the boardwalk, giving them an idea of what animals live in the land around the bay. The boardwalk goes on for some way and comes to an intersection where you can go right through the tall marsh grass

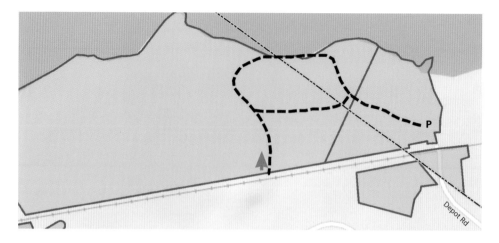

and use a mounted viewing lens to look out across the water. When the ducks and geese are migrating down the Atlantic Coast, you can see many different species resting in the bay. Other birds along with eagles and osprey make their homes here. I once saw a golden eagle soar overhead right at the tree line above us while duck hunting on the other side of the bay. A beautiful and bountiful natural area.

Follow the boardwalk around and after it turns and heads back, take the right onto the trail that goes past the wigwam onto sold ground. A short walk further and, if you keep a lookout for a Big Tree, the black oak will show itself a little off the trail on the left. Its wide bottom makes it look huge and the neat-looking bark draws you in. The little hole going in at the bottom lets you know there is some heart rot, but overall, it seems to be in good shape. This tree, along with many big trees you may have seen, has an advantage over some of the others. It has been near the RR tracks and open sunlight just a bit longer, so it has grown faster and made its niche here work for it.

When going back out, look for some of the other species of oak to help with your ID skills. There are white and red oaks along with some gum, elm, and birch.

Difficulty 1   Great for kids. Close to RR tracks though, so watch them.

133" CBH 78' VH 69' ACS   Total Points 228   Good Condition
GPS: N 43.054210° W 070.901020°

Directions

From Route 33 in Stratham, take Depot Road and follow it to the end. Go left and cross the RR tracks to the Great Bay Discovery Center.

Exeter Tree Tour

This small town is a great place to visit with a line of storefronts on Water Street and with the Swazey Parkway, a beautiful grassy park along the river where the farmers market, concerts, and special events are held during the summer. You can visit one of several restaurants in town, or for an outside lunch visit a sandwich shop and get takeout to eat while sitting along the waterfront. Known as the birthplace of the Republican Party, the town has hosted many prominent politicians, including Abraham Lincoln, whose son attended Phillips Exeter Academy, the school that is still known as one of the best prep schools on the East Coast.

A nice biking or walking tour can start at the Swazey Parkway with two state champions to get you going. One, a river birch, that is across from the bandstand, is important for those who want to understand this

State champ pin oak — Peace.

Looking over the pitch pine.

tree. It is a transplant in NH, and you will see it planted at some auto dealers lots and storefronts in many towns. Most of what you see are the younger trees, which have loose, curly bark that is peeling off with a yellow and brown color. The birches in this park are much older and have much darker, thicker bark with a reddish tint. I have not seen as many river birches of the size that you will see along the sidewalk from here into town anywhere in northern New England. This birch has recently had one of its forked trunks cut that was hanging over the house nearby. On both sides of the road as you head toward town there are two pin oaks, very similar in size, that compete for state champ. The telltale feature of this tree is the deeply lobed leaves and the pin ends giving it its name. This is another that is not native to the area but planted because of its impressive looks. The one closest to the river on the grassy area provides excellent shade and is a refuge for those enjoying the park on a hot summer day.

Go out of the parkway and head right on Main Street and look at the American elm next to the sidewalk near the house on the right. This is the second largest in Rockingham County and has a wide spreading crown that arches over the house and road. The Independence Museum is across the street and you could wander over there to look around. If you plan your trip on a July weekend you could visit the same day as their British-French military reenactments.

About a third of a mile further up Main Street, take a left on Lincoln Street and go for about ¼ mile, then turn right on Garfield going around to the end past the Agway store. Cross Front Street and go right to Arbor Street and into the cemetery.

This is an old cemetery with many graves of prominent NH citizens and a few Big Trees. Take a good look at the former county champ Norway spruce, then, on the far side, you will come to some impressive pitch pines. These trees were once called candlewood because they were used as a light source in colonial days. The resin in the branches would burn for some time, making them the best trees to use for that purpose. The county champ is here with a circumference of 104".

Head out to the other end of the cemetery and keep a lookout for other large trees but stay on the sidewalk and off private property while heading back on Front Street.

Keep going to the center of town and back to where you parked to finish your two-mile loop to see the trees. Be sure to save time to visit some of the shops, maybe a restaurant, and the local bookstore to top off your day.

Difficulty Rating 2

1. River Birch

123" CBH   50' VH   77' ACS   Total Points 192   Good Condition
GPS: N 42.984783°   W 70.951312°
Δ State Champion

2. Pin Oak

157" CBH   92' VH   86' ACS   Total Points 271   Excellent Condition
GPS: N 42.984031°   W 70.950501°
Δ State Champion

3. Pin Oak

170 " CBH   80' VH   89' ACS   Total Points 272   Excellent Condition
GPS: N 42.983810°   W 70.950087°
Δ State Champion

4. American Elm

156" CBH   71' VH   72' ACS   Total Points 245   Good Condition
GPS: N 42.981686°   W 70.951004°

5. Norway Spruce

135" CBH   89' VH   61' ACS   Total Points 239   Excellent Condition
GPS: N 42.976250° W 70.960467°

6. Norway Spruce

159" CBH   76' VH   67' ACS   Total Points 252   Good Condition
GPS: N 42.975131° W 70.961665°

7. Pitch Pine

104" CBH   78' VH   56' ACS   Total Points 196   Good Condition
GPS: N 42.975367° W 70.961169°

Δ County Champion

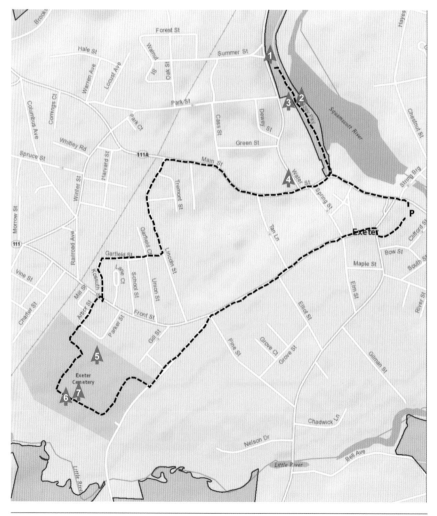

American Beech *[Fagus grandifolia]*

T he Burley and Chase families owned this farm and woodland for generations. The last owners, Nancy Chase and Jane Burley, who have been very conservation minded Epping residents, opted to protect the land forever by selling it at a discounted price to the Southeast Land Trust of NH. The 237 acres is open to the public for passive recreational uses such as hiking, snowshoeing, and hunting. It includes a large beaver pond and connects to other blocks of protected land along the nationally designated Wild and Scenic Lamprey River. Nearing completion as this book is written is the Mathey Center for People and Nature, which will offer a destination for field trips and outdoor adventures, nature-based education for children and adults, and community groups looking to gather against the backdrop of this sprawling scenic vista. In addition, the historic John Prescott Chase Farmhouse (located across from the Mathey Center) will be revitalized to provide workforce housing, and the working farm will soon spring back to life.

Our main interest now is with the trails that border the fields and go off into the woods. The state champion American beech stands not too far from the parking area along the stonewall on the fields western edge. The American beech is a very common tree in northern New England and often grows in nearly pure stands. The young trees can grow tightly together with branches whipping against you as you try to make your way through them. These tight stands provide cover for wildlife, with the leaves and buds foraged for food while the larger, more mature trees nearby provide small, nutritious nuts for deer and bears, who sometimes depend on these nuts to fatten up and get through the winter. The beech can be a beautiful tree with its smooth steel gray bark and full crown. The leaves turn an orange yellow color in the fall, and all winter some trees will have the dead leaves hang on making a welcome rustling noise in the wind on a cold snowy day. This tree is hollow, and although the bark is mottled and not smooth, that is likely from old age and not the fungus that is killing most of the beech in NH. A smoother example that is an American beech at 107" circumference is located just a little further down the trail.

Beech lumber is not often used but can make good furniture and is

State champ beech.

used for dowels, clothespins, and other small wooden items. The leaves can be boiled in water and eaten when fresh in the spring. A coffee can be made from the nuts in the fall. Gather them and cook at 300° in the oven for 15 to 30 minutes to crack the shell. Shell them, dry the nuts further in the oven until brittle, then grind them until like coffee. Steep a teaspoon in boiling water for 15 minutes. Could also be mixed with regular coffee.

Make your way around the field for a short loop walk, and on the other side is a hemlock that is part of a tree line that separates the fields. This was either a fort for some kids at one time or a tree stand, as you can see the rungs nailed on the trunk so it could be climbed. It has a decent circumference for a hemlock and should keep growing fairly fast in its open location. From here, if you want a longer walk, you can follow the trail around the other field out to North River Road and find the trail again on the right that goes into the next field and then along the old French Road to the woods behind that. It loops around the woodland, then back the way you came. For a longer day trip, you can take French Road down where it meets Dimond Hill Road and the unmarked trails to the Lamprey River or over to the North River.

On one winter trip to this property, we saw an almost all white bird of prey that likely was a young snowy owl, so I will have to associate this tree with them. It landed in a small tree in the middle of the field. They like to hunt mice, voles, and small birds in open farmland areas like this.

Difficulty Rating 1

American Beech

134" CBH   108' VH   69' ACS   Total Points 259   Fair Condition
GPS: N 43.061464°   W 71.043968°
Δ State Champion

Eastern Hemlock

139" CBH   78.5' VH   56' ACS   Total Points 231   Good Condition
GPS: N 43.064354°   W 71.044490°

Directions

From Route 101 in Epping, take 125 North about 2.5 miles and just after the Route 87 intersection look for North River Road on the right. Take that about a ⅓ of a mile to a right at the entrance to Burley Farms.

Black Walnut *[Juglans nigra L.]*

The Goodrich farm homestead is at this site in Pawtuckaway State Park, where you can see old foundations, a well head, a cemetery, and a very wide-crowned black walnut. This is likely not native and must have been planted by the family to supply them with nuts to add to their baked goods at a time when a trip to the supermarket was not an option. We are at the northern edge of this type's range, and it was heavily cut in the 1800s because of its value as lumber. Luckily, it was frequently planted in the northern climates at homes in the city or country. It is rare to find them in the woods, though, and this one may be helping to repopulate the area, with several young walnut trees growing nearby. The lumber from these trees is the most valuable of all our woods and the veneer logs can be worth upwards of $1,000. It is used for fine furniture, cabinetry, and gunstocks. I have used the wood

Jerry Langdon and black walnut.

for some small jewelry boxes and it has a nice reddish-brown appearance and a grain similar to mahogany though quite a bit heavier in weight. In the summer, you can drive right up tower road to the walnut with no hike involved. You could make it a starting point and then hike up to the tower on South Mountain or take the Middle Mountain Trail just across the brook. In the winter, the tower road is gated, so you can park near the beginning and then snowshoe or ski along on the snowmobile trail that follows the road. You pass the edge of a small pond, and, after crossing a brook, you will see the tree on the right. The home at this site was owned by the Goodrich family and you can see their graves in the cemetery nearby. The barn foundation is behind the walnut tree and the well is off to the other side.

The Goodriches were early settlers who had six children and a hard early life. Their daughter died at two years old. Then several years later, they lost four sons and the father to smallpox. You can see their graves in the cemetery. The surviving son lived there with his wife and the mother. He had one child who eventually took over the farm when his grandmother passed at 101 years old. He was a bit eccentric and never wore shoes, getting the name the Barefoot Farmer from the locals in Raymond where he sold his goods. He was also a photographer and took many photos, some showing this very walnut tree next to his farmhouse. He loved the land here and, having no heirs, he gave the land to the state to help form Pawtuckaway State Park.

While a few of the other walnuts in Rockingham County are larger, the others are in front or back yards and do not have the same appeal that this has. We can say that this one has the largest crown of all the walnuts in the state. With its 111' spread, it takes up a bit of room on the hillside of the Pawtuckaway woods.

Difficulty 2

132" CBH   81' VH   111' ACS   Total Points 241   Good Condition
GPS: N 43.105720°   W 071.183270°

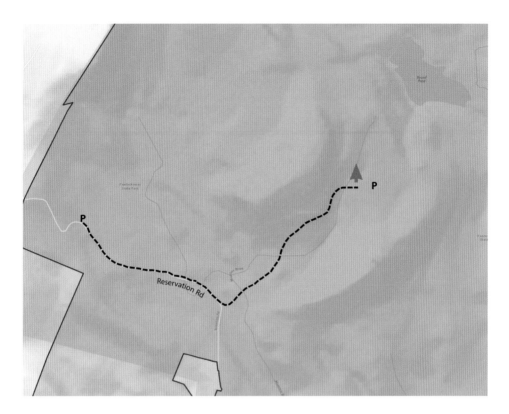

Directions

From Route 107 in Deerfield, take Reservation Road toward the tower at Pawtuckaway State Park. The road will turn dirt continue past Round Pond Road on the left. You can pass the tree site to park at the tower trail parking area and walk a few hundred feet back to the walnut. In the winter, park where you can near the gate, at the beginning of Tower Road. This is a well-used park so if you want to avoid the crowds come in the middle of the week or during the off season.

Blue Hills Range Hemlock

The Blue Hills range includes an exceptional block of conserved forestland in Southeastern NH. The hills of the range are Evans Mt, Parker Mt, Mack Mt, Sanders Ledge, and Blue Job Mt—a popular small mountain for hiking with a fire tower at the top. Huckins Brook and Big River run through the conserved lands. Many swamps and other wetlands are found here near the old roads, with the foundations from some of the homesteads in view as you walk along. The Bear Paw Regional Greenway and the Blue Hills Foundation worked together to conserve some of the land. George Lovejoy, whose career was in the Boston area real estate field, summered his whole life in the Blue Hills area and grew to love it. He started to purchase land to save it from development in the 1960s and through the Blue Hills Foundation continued to help conserve the land here until his recent death. This 16,000-acre woodland area is separated by Route 126 from another 6,000-acre block that together provide a permanent home for the bears, moose, bobcats, and other wildlife that need these large tracts of land to thrive. This shows some of the great strides southern NH has taken to protect its special natural features.

Big River view.

County champ hemlock.

From the parking area at the end of Little Niagra Falls Road, head past the gate and cross the culvert at Big River while enjoying that beautiful view. Cut through on a small, unmarked hard-to-see trail a short distance to an old woods road. Follow that road for some distance, keeping the wetland of Big River in a distance on your left. Head uphill a bit and stay on the main trail. Your GPS will come in handy on this trip, so punch in the tree coordinates before you start to help out. It would be a good idea to have the parking coordinates to get back, too. You keep following trails going up again and cresting the top, then heading down. Once you come to a small ravine with an intermittent stream that may be dry, start following it up. It will get steeper as you go but should be manageable with no real climbing or rock scrambling involved. Maybe ¾ of the way up, start looking to the left and the tree will come into view near the top of that side. This hemlock is the Strafford County champ for the species. It has a good circumference but is not too tall.

At one time, the largest deer wintering area in southern NH was thought to be in the hemlock woods that were in this block of land. Most of the timber was cut at some point, but pockets were left that provide the protection the deer herd needs to survive the harsh snowy winters. The thick hemlock woods with all its fully needled branches will collect the snow and keep the depth down so the deer can get around after the big storms. They will also feed on the twigs and needles until the snow pack goes down.

The bobcat is also plentiful here and rebounding in NH. A hunting season was proposed, but the public spoke out against it and it was voted down, allowing their numbers to continue to increase. A few years ago, one crossed the highway in front of me while I was heading up Route 16 outside of Rochester in NH. A large and handsome example that was impressive to see. These large ones will take deer frequently, while smaller cats will if they can but mostly live off smaller mammals like squirrels and hares. I think I will associate this tree with the bobcat that I can imagine resting under this hemlock while looking over the small ravine below.

Difficulty Rating 4   Need GPS.

144" CBH   75.5' VH   45' ACS   Total Points 231   Good Condition
GPS: N 43.32190°   W 71.13766°
Δ Strafford County Champion

Directions

From 202A, take first Crown Point Road and continue past the Blue Job Mountain parking area at just under 5 miles to the turn for Little Niagra Falls Road at about 6 miles. Continue on Little Niagra Falls about ¼ mile to a parking area at the end. Parking: N 43.33155°   W 71.15054°

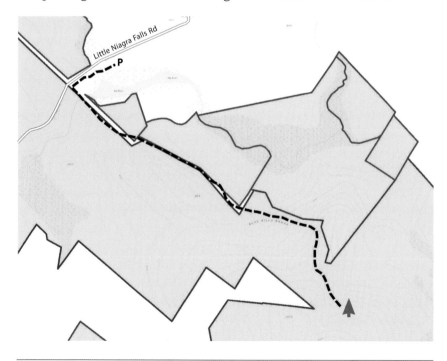

Chestnut Oak *[Quercus prinus L.]*

T his type of oak is not frequently found in my area of southeastern New Hampshire or in southern Maine but is more common in southwestern NH. Its distribution is limited in the state with red, black, and white oaks more widely found. A trip to the Mile Slip Town Forest in Milford will provide a hike along Mitchell Brook with its hillside full of mountain laurel and to the state champion chestnut oak. This 452-acre forest, in the wildest part of Milford, connects with other protected lands, providing almost 7,000 acres of conserved land for use by the public and provides home for wildlife that include bear, bobcat, and moose that need more forestland to roam around in. Besides the white pine and red oak, the forestry plan for the property shows chestnut oak as providing the third-largest timber amount on the land.

The hike starts off from the parking area and follows the SN 501 trail down to catch the class 6 Mile Slip Road for a bit. Then you look for a right turn into the woods, following the Mitchell Brook Trail with

Chestnut oak and measurers.

Mountain laurels in bloom.

its white trail markers. You will start to see some chestnut oak here and there with its chunky bark and the chestnut-tree-shaped leaves that give it its name. Also very noticeable are the mountain laurel bushes that are spread throughout. I have fought through some dense and almost impenetrable, tightly packed mountain laurel in wetter areas while trying to get to some black gum trees to measure. Here it is on dryer land and spreads along the sides of the trail. In the winter, their conspicuous evergreen leaves add some greenery down at eye level. If you plan your trip in early June, they may be in full bloom and add quite a bit of sensory enhancement to your visit.

As you continue along the trail, the state champ chestnut oak will soon show itself. This gnarly-looking tree has lost some large branches which healed over into large burls going up the tree, and two are right at normal circumference-measuring height of 4.5 feet. We measured above and below the swelling wood around these long-gone branches and determined which was best to go by, deciding upon the lower measurement because the upper one was influenced by a large missing branch on the backside. This tree must have grown in the open farm or grazing land that once occurred here, with large lower branches spreading sideways in the sun until the forest started growing back around it shading and killing off the lower branches.

Chestnut oak is considered a part of the white oaks group, whose acorns mature in one year and have rounded leaf lobes. Besides the chestnut oak, this group includes burr oak, swamp white oak, and white oak. The black/red oak group have sharp lobes and their acorns take two years to mature. The lumber is said to be similar to white oak and can be used for the same purposes, so at times they are mixed in lumberyards. I have not knowingly used chestnut oak but have on occasion used white oak that I thought was stringier than normal, so perhaps that was chestnut oak.

After your visit, continue along the Mitchell Brook Trail and follow the brook with its darker hemlock and pine woods uphill and pass by a few benches along the stream. If you keep a lookout, a few pines show up on the right and a little off the trail that looked pretty good-sized, so it might be worth checking their circumference. The trail keeps going up along the dry soil here for another ½ mile or so to the parking area.

Difficulty Rating 2

188" CBH   82' VH   56' ACS   Total Points 284   Fair Condition
GPS: N 42.781964°   W 071.712308°
Δ State Champion

Directions

From 101 in Milford, take Route 13 to Armory Road, following it to the end then turning right on Osgood and then left onto Mason Road. Follow that about 2.25 miles and go left on Mile Slip Road, which makes its way through newer housing on a narrower and narrower winding road. It turns into a solid dirt road till it ends at a parking area for the town forest, then it turns to a class 6 road from there.

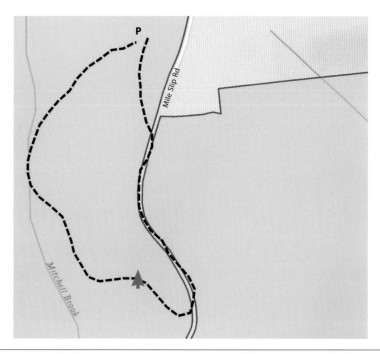

38 *Washington*

Washington Red Spruce

Take this out-of-the-way woodland trek if you need an adventure that includes a small town, dirt roads, a pond, and a bushwhack to one of the largest red spruces in western NH. Washington is one of those classic New England towns with the white town office buildings and church at its center, and a very rural cluster of country houses surrounding that center. The dirt roads start right from the town hall, with Halfmoon Pond Road going out past the pond and into the Max Israel State Forest where the tree is located. While waiting at the town hall parking area, I saw a hiker come out from behind the building and then saw him later way down the road. Turns out the Monadnock-Sunapee Greenway goes right through town and down the road until it turns off onto the Lovewell Mountain trail.

As you drive from town, you continue past the pond and Lovewell Mountain Road. You eventually come to a sign saying it's a class 6

Foresters Billy Kunelius and William Guinn at red spruce.

unmaintained road. It got rocky and bumpy but was passable with my two-wheel-drive pickup truck. If you have a vehicle with low clearance, you may not want to take the road any further. If you can find a spot off the road here, you can park and walk the mile or so to the clearing that a higher vehicle would park at. You are now in the Max Israel State Forest. This is managed by state foresters and they keep wildlife and recreational needs in mind when cutting the woods to encourage regrowth of certain species. The forester, Billy Kunelius, who manages state forests in the southern part of the state, found this spruce along with a few others of good size and thought it was worth entering into the NH Big Tree Program to ensure this tree is noted and kept around for us to see. Red spruce and balsam fir are spread throughout, reminding me of the woods you find in the far northern part of the state. This more southern area is cold enough with a snow belt through here encouraging them to grow.

From the small clearing, take the logging road on the right for about a ½ mile and then bushwhack to the GPS coordinates for the spruce. As you are walking, take note of the trees you see on the sides of the road. Most are young hardwood regrowth from logging in the past. We saw moose tracks on the road and droppings near the big spruce, another sign that wildlife is as attracted to these Big Trees as we humans are. I think we can associate this tree with the moose that seem abundant in the area. The forester said partridge, which are much less common now in my area of coastal NH, are also seen frequently in these forests.

When bushwhacking, you will cross a small brook that was completely dry the drought year that we crossed it but should be easily managed when fully running. The woods are easy to walk through and before long you come to the red spruce. We wondered why this tree was left here to grow to the size it is. Usually, they are left because they are in a hard to get at spot in steep rocky areas. That may be where the few other big spruce are located that the forester said are on this land not too far away. This one must have been left at the whim of the logger or land owners of the past. You can tell by the lower dead branches that this tree was growing for a while in an open landscape. Most large spruces I have measured did not have the lower branches like this because they grew from the start in a more forested, mountainous part of the state. With a circumference of 92.4", it's among the top spruce trees in NH and in this setting makes a great morning or afternoon outing. To enjoy the area more, you could spend the rest of the day going up Lovewell Mountain or paddling around Halfmoon Pond.

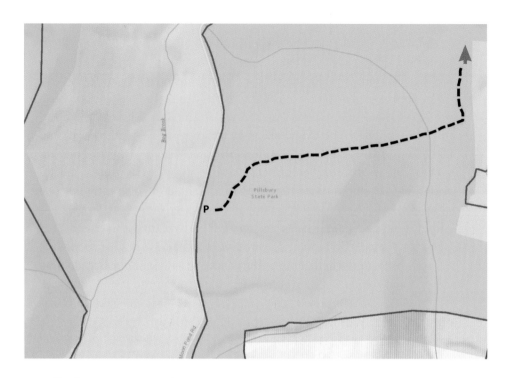

Difficulty rating 3   Need GPS.

92" CBH   83' VH   30' ACS   Total Points 183   Good Condition
GPS: N 43.222198°   W 072.064273°
Δ Sullivan County Champion

Directions

From Route 31 in the center of Washington, take the dirt Halfmoon Pond Road that leaves from the town hall. In just over a ½ mile, go left staying on Halfmoon Pond Road where it meets Mill Road and go 2.5 miles to Martin Road. From there, stay on Halfmoon Pond Road, go as far as you can and find a place to park off the road. We parked about a mile further and walked from there. It likely won't be plowed in the winter and you'll need a GPS to find tree.

Furthest parking: GPS: N 43.220193°   W 072.076060°

Black Cherry *[Prunus serotina]*

Chesterfield, NH, is a town that takes pride in its woodlands. The conservation commission along with others in the area have worked to conserve properties for wildlife and recreational uses. They have a nice website with trail maps showing where visitors can go to enjoy the outdoors. On the Madam Sherry property, remaining stonework includes the famous "staircase to nowhere," which partially collapsed in 2021. Sherry's estate has an interesting history that you may want to research. Chesterfield Gorge is a small thirteen-acre state park off Route 9 that includes a deep gorge cut by the Wild River with trails along its sides. Nearby them both is the Freidsam Town Forest, which is the draw for Big Tree enthusiasts. The Big Trees are highlighted in their trail map of this land, with a few large oaks on one end of the site and one of the state's most impressive black cherry trees on the other end. The 1.8-mile Sargent Trail goes through to the cherry, making a 3.6-mile out and back trip with a side trip on the Ancient Oaks Trail to view the oaks. A loop trip could be made by connecting to the Ancient

Cherry and measuring crew.

Oaks Trail via the Cemetery Trail at the far end. For a shorter walk, you can start at the end of the Sargent Trail closest to the cherry and make a short out and back walk of it. Then drive to the other parking area and walk out and back to the oaks. Starting from the furthest parking area from Route 9, off Twin Brook Road, begin by walking down to one of the Twin Brooks. Cross the nicely built small bridge and you may see some of a beaver's industrious labor on the right. After a little up-hill walking, by some smaller cherry trees you will pass what is shown on the map as the great ash, which is now dead. Which of the trees around it will grow to be the next great tree, I wonder? A little further and the cherry we came to see shows up.

The black cherry has brownish, flaking bark that gives off a pleasant aroma after a rain, as do the flowers or fruit at certain times of the year. Sawing or sanding the lumber makes my shop smell good for a few days, and it's one of the best woods to work with. It works easily with hand tools, finishes much better than the more open-grain woods like oak or ash, and turns a nice reddish-brown with age. I can almost see that color on the bark of this gem of a tree. The wood is prized by furniture builders, and I use it for decks, gunwales, and other trim on some of my lapstrake canoes. At times, I will re-saw boards 14" to 16" wide as book-matched decking for my long-decked courting canoes. In New England, most cherry trees grow crooked or branch out early, so our trees are not as good for lumber as the trees in Pennsylvania, where they are managed to grow straight and tall. My father gave me some cherry he brought back from his father's farm sawmill in Tennessee. I used it for some furniture and made wooden spoons for Christmas gifts for family members, noting where it came from. Future family heirlooms, I hope.

You can imagine how the wildlife are attracted to the cherry fruit. Songbirds of all types flock to the berries in the fall, eating the berries and excreting the seeds in the nearby woods, spreading the cherry trees around. In the past, the seeds would get dispersed around the open farmland and the wilted leaves were poisonous to farm animals, so farmers would often cut the trees. I have bought the cherry lumber cut along the fence lines or boundaries of local farms close to me. The farms are getting scarce now though, so maybe we should encourage more forest-grown cherry in the area. I don't think many NH woods are managed with cherry in mind.

To enjoy this property some more, continue on by foot or go back to your vehicle and see some ancient oaks.

Difficulty Rating 3

Cherry

154" CBH   85' VH   45' ACS   Total Points 250   Fair Condition
GPS: N 42.895099°   W 072.468019°
Δ Cheshire County Champion

Red oak

201" CBH   97' VH   80' ACS   Total Points 318   Excellent Condition
GPS: N 42.901787°   W 072.473427°
Δ Cheshire County Champion

Directions

From Route 9 in Chesterfield, get on Twin Brooks Road. Go a short distance to the parking area on the left. If you want to make a longer hike out of this visit, you can park at the first parking area to see the ancient oak and hike to the cherry. For a shorter hike, you can park just under a mile down the road and start there.

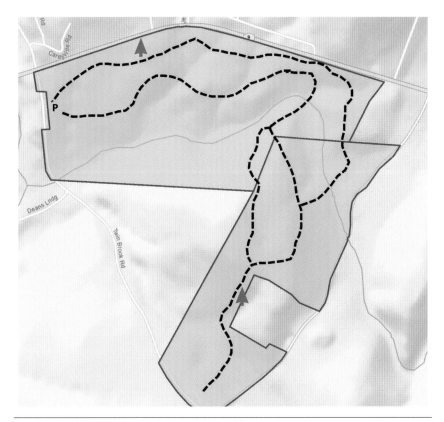

Honeylocust *[Gleditsia triacanthos L.]*

Consider yourself lucky to be looking at this tree on such an important property in Cornish. This was the home of the sculptor Augustus Saint Gaudens, who is considered as one of the greatest artists this country has produced. His work is amazing, with several national treasures to his name. You can see some of these and working models of others here at the estate: The Adams memorial is a mournful statue. The Farragut Monument of famous Civil War Admiral David Glascow Farragut is also there. The monument was made for New York City and unveiled at Madison Square Park in 1881. The original base is now here with a recasting of the statue on top, The most impressive to me is a casting of the original Shaw Memorial, which is located in Boston. This sculpture depicts a group of African-American soldiers knowingly marching to their deaths with movement, feelings, and mood all showing in this still piece of art.

The Cornish Colony included several other artists and craftsmen who summered in this area at the turn of the twentieth century, including Maxfield Parish, who was just down the road. His former home has a state champion white oak which he included in some of his artwork. It is on private land, so you can't visit that tree but a photo is included in the book.

Shaw Memorial.

Honeylocust.

From the parking lot at the St. Gaudens National Historic Site, pay the entrance fee, walk through the hedges, and you will immediately see the state champion—and for a short time the national champion— thornless honeylocust. It was planted 134 years ago in 1886 when Augustus St. Gaudens moved into the home year-round. Sitting on the hill at the entrance to the home, it draws awe as you walk close by. It shades the house, keeping things cooler, and has benches underneath for guests to use.

The honeylocust can be recognized by its compound, alternate leaf stems with 18 to 28 leaflets on each. Unlike our black locust, which spreads easily, these trees are planted for the most part and seen around homes or estates. While this one is thornless, some varieties have thorns that can be 3" long on the branches and trunk. Locust is known as a very rot-resistant wood; I have used it for posts for a kiosk frame describing some conserved land in Epping and for boat frames in dories and wherries. Its wood has a greenish look, so would contrast with darker woods when used for small, wooden items.

If you want, you can start from the Visitor's Center instead of going right up to the tree and combine some culture with your tree viewing.

Mt. Ascutney from side yard.

From the center, you can go through some of the building with pictures, history exhibits, some sculptures, along with an atrium. Then work your way to the impressive Shaw Memorial that was commissioned to show the strength and courage of a black regiment marching to their certain death in a battle against overwhelming odds during the Civil War.

Go on to see the emotional Adams Memorial that St. Gaudens called "The mystery of the hereafter and beyond pain." It was commissioned by Henry Adams for his wife, who for many years was mourning the loss of their son. To brighten things back up, go past the back of the house through the flower gardens to catch a view of Mt. Ascutney lurking behind the corner of the house, then go out front again to see the honeylocust.

To make a hike out of the visit, continue on across the expansive lawns to find the trailhead to Blow Me Down Brook. On the loop you can see two pines that grew quite tall. There are some others nearby in Paradise Park on the Windsor, VT, side of the Connecticut River, too. Apparently, the river valley is great for growing Big Trees.

Difficulty Rating 2 With loop to Blow Me Down Brook.

HoneyLocust

201" CBH   99' VH   91' ACS   Total Points 323   Excellent Condition
GPS: N 43.500500°   W 072.369180°
Δ State Champion

Eastern White Pine

132" CBH   130' VH   44' ACS   Total Points 273   Excellent Condition
GPS: N 43.501670°   W 072.378680°

2nd Pine

132" CBH   130' VH   No crown spread measured.   Good Condition
GPS: N 43.500580°   W 072.374270°

Directions

From I-89 in West Lebanon, take 12A south for about 11.5 miles and take a sharp left onto St. Gaudens Road. Follow it ½ a mile to the estate on the left.

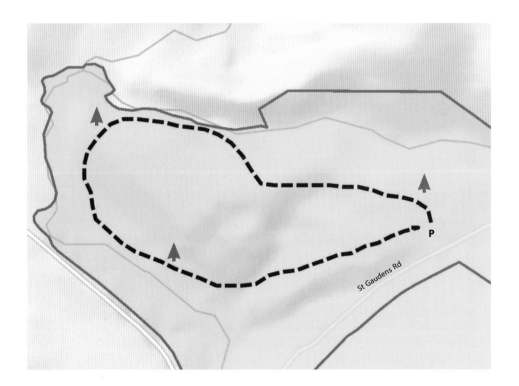

Dartmouth Tree Tour

Hanover is home of the well-known Dartmouth College campus that encompasses much of the town. As with many other colleges, trees have been planted around the grounds to provide shade and comfort for the students. The elms are foremost here and should be noted for their number and size as best in all of northern New England. The streets were lined with them as fresh plantings in the late 1800s and now they've grown large enough to be called Big Trees. Brian

State champion elm. Photo by Brian Beaty.

State champ Norway spruce and arborist Scott Melendy.

Beaty, the lead arborist for the college showed us some of their awesome trees, including four state champions: a Kentucky coffeetree, Norway spruce, Camperdown elm, and American elm. Also on the campus are a yellowwood, a Japanese larch, and a special memorial to the infamous Dartmouth pine at the top of the hill at College Park.

With its setting in western NH, the alumni have over the years been known for their outdoor pursuits, with the Dartmouth Outing Club active in hiking, skiing, rowing, and other outdoor activities. In 1807, the second College Grant lands were given to the college by the state. Located north of Erroll and Lake Umbago, it consists of 2,700 acres of forests and recreational land. The land has been managed for timber as an income source and has natural areas set aside with nearby cabins for use by students and alumni. I'm not sure of the size of the trees up there currently, but in the 1870s a pine was reported to have been cut near the Dead Dimond River that measured 7'4" in diameter at the butt and 3'1" at 90' up, yielding 1,200 feet of lumber. You can see several good-sized pines while in Hanover at Pine Park, with trails along Girl Brook and the Connecticut River.

Find parking in the center of town and head down North Main Street to Tuck Mall or Tuck Road. The Kentucky coffeetree is on the corner. Named for the use of its seeds as a substitute for coffee in the colonial

Dartmouth pine memorial and tower.

days, it's native to the Midwest and is a good urban tree planted in northern states for its drought tolerance and good looks. The leaves are different shades in the spring and yellowish in the fall, with the female holding its contrasting brown seed pods into the winter. The lumber is used for furniture and cabinets in areas where it's common.

Continue down the mall and between McKlane Hall and Butterfield Hall you can't miss the state champion American elm. This tree is starting to show its age, with dead wood on parts of the trunk and its likely quite hollow. That signature vase shape that made it so popular to plant in many towns shows plainly here and on several other elms on the campus. Keep an eye out for them, as many here are in great shape, with some naturally resistant to Dutch elm disease and others treated to prevent it.

Further on down the Tuck Mall Road, bear right to Old Tuck Drive and up on the road bank on the right side a Norway spruce will come into view. Beyond the fence is the home of the president of the college, so be respectful while viewing the tree. It has an impressive circumference and a large swooping branch coming out above your head. This one and another in NH that is tied for state champion are larger than any others measured in northern New England.

Go back the way you came and over to the corner of West Wheelock Street and North Main Street and you can view another tree that is native to the state of Kentucky, a yellowwood. These are known for clusters of fragrant white flowers in the spring and yellow leaves in the fall. It is a medium-sized tree that won't grow so large as to overpower the landscape near the buildings. Cross Wheelock Street and go south on Main Street a few blocks, then go left onto South Street. Follow that to the end, then go left on Sanborn Road and in front of a college-owned home is the state champion camperdown elm. These cool-looking trees are prized as landscape trees, and I think you can see why, with its short, rugged stature and nice spreading crown. Please respect those living at the building and try to stay on the sidewalk.

For a look at another side of the college, follow Sanborn north past the St. Denis Catholic Church and cross Lebanon Street past Memorial Field on Crosby Street. Cross East Wheelock Street to Observatory Road and find your way to a path going behind Ripley Hall into the wooded College Park. On the lower end near an outdoor theater among the trees, you can find a Japanese larch. This tree differs slightly from the European version, with its cones and different-colored twigs. Head up the hill to the top to find a stone observation tower and a memorial to the Old Pine that was a guardian of the traditions of the college. It was struck by lightning in 1887 and after a whirlwind in 1892 had to be cut, with a replacement planted in 1912. I hope this is a fitting end to your tour and helps you see how a college that turns out some of the best doctors in the world has also shown respect and appreciation of the special trees we have around us.

Difficulty 1

1. Kentucky coffetree

105" CBH   91' VH   64.50 ACS   Total Points 212   Fair Condition
GPS: N 43.704940°   W 72.289870°
Δ State Champion

2. American Elm

197" CBH   93' VH   109' ACS   Total Points 317   Fair Condition
GPS: N 43.705435°   W 72.291144°
Δ State Champion

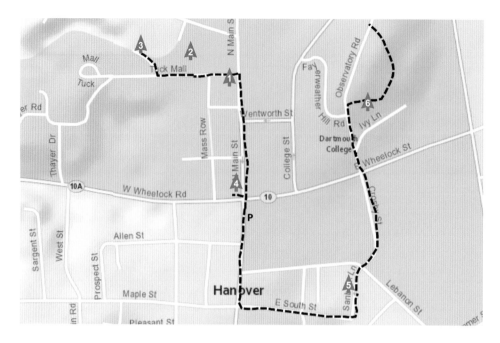

3. Norway Spruce

186" CBH   115' VH   40' ACS   Total Points 311   Good Condition
GPS: N 43.705779° W 72.293249°
Δ State Champion

4. Yellowwood

No Measurements

5. Camperdown Elm

108' C   23' VH   39' ACS   Total Points 141   Poor Condition
GPS: N 43.700262° W 72.286024°
Δ State Champion

6. Japanese Larch

119" CBH   118' VH   38' ACS   Total Points 246   Excellent Condition
 GPS: N 43.704693° W 72.284741°
Δ State co-champion

Directions

From I-89, take 120 toward Hanover. Go 4.2 miles and bear right onto
South Park Street. Go just under a ½ mile and turn left onto East Wheelock Street and to the center of town to find parking.

Big Red

A visit to this tree would be a good addition to the day of touring the Dartmouth campus. Just down the road a few miles from the college, it's a change of scenery with a woods walk to the Boston Lot Lake and up Honeysuckle Hill to the oak tree that is nicknamed Big Red. The Boston Lot is part of over four hundred acres of conserved land surrounding the pond and owned by the town of Lebanon. It was named the Boston Lot because in the late 1800s a company from Boston had planned to mine its pink granite since its location close to the Connecticut River allowed for easy shipping to the south. Years later, the pond was made and for some time was used as a water source for the City of Lebanon. Trails come to the pond from several directions, with the most prominent starting from a parking area along Route 10 near the Wilder Dam.

From the kiosk, head up Honeysuckle Hill following a stream you can see down in a small ravine. Not too far along this wide trail that looks kept in shape for vehicle access, you come to a sign near the top

Big Red and me.

showing the trails. I mistakenly followed a trail from there that started with an orange blaze on a tree that matched the orange color I saw on the kiosk below for the Honeysuckle Trail. This was not the Honeysuckle Trail, so if you want to keep your visit short, continue on past the sign to the fork in the wide tote road trail and find the real Honeysuckle Loop. For a bit longer hike and to view a few other big oaks, you can take the wrong trail down toward and into view of the powerlines. You will circumnavigate the hill and can come in on the other side to see Big Red, or you can go back the way you came and up to the top. If following the lower trail, the first big oak you see will be lying beside the trail and was quite impressive in its time. This gives you an idea of how these dead trees are used by wildlife and insects until they are turned back into the soil from which they came. Go on a bit further and to your left about 75 feet or so into the woods another one is standing, almost dead, but I saw one live branch still hanging on. It's close in size to Big Red at the top. The red oaks seem to thrive here with more sunlight and better growing conditions near the Connecticut River, as many are good-sized. They also may have been managed for their growth as special silviculture practices were said to be used at one time on this land. As you walk this trail, be sure to keep an eye out for some bitternut hickory that for the most part only grows along the Connecticut River in NH. I turned around here and went back the way I came. If you keep going and meet the Sachem Village Trail then head back up on the other side of the hill, you may see some other trees worth pondering, then try to meet up with the trail to the top.

The Honeysuckle Loop Trail starts out of a clearing off Westside Trail and heads up to the top of the hill. Not too far up, you will come to Big Red. I like saying that. It's in quite a bit better condition than the other one lower down, but it's still in rough shape, with a hollow center and dead main branches. These red oaks are a boon to the local wildlife for their acorns. Some animals likely continue to visit them all year as an old friend who will be there to help them in hard times. In the winter, you have a bit of a view of Burnt Mountain from here, but much of the year other trees will block the view. Walk on and around the loop to see why it's called Honeysuckle Hill. The plants grow in abundance as you go on and flower at certain times of the year, providing an enjoyable walk around the hilltop. After the loop, don't miss the short trail that brings you to the Boston Lot Lake with its views all year. Take a loop around it if time allows and look for other interesting trees.

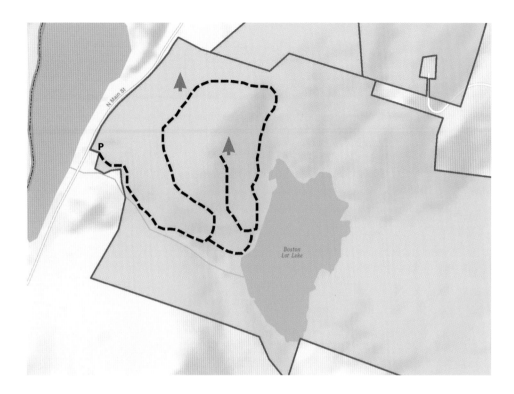

Difficulty Rating 3

Almost dead oak

196" CBH   71' VH
GPS: N 43.67059°   W 72.29629°

Big Red

205.8" CBH   78' VH   44.66' ACS   Total Points 295   Poor Condition
GPS: N 43.66770°   W 72.29377°

Directions

From I-89 in Lebanon, take Route 10 North for 1.25 miles to the parking
area on the right across from the dam.

Big Tree Growth Rates

In New Hampshire, the Big Tree Program has been keeping track of the measurements of trees taken from the 1960s and comparing them to our current measurements. Other studies have also been done, and a chart was made giving an idea of the growth rate of Big Trees so we can extrapolate a rough age from a circumference. The studies were of forest-grown trees, and there would be differences with open-grown or city trees. Our program may help give a better idea of the differences by keeping track of all the trees we have listed. The chart below was taken from the other forested setting studies, so keep that in mind when trying to determine the age of a tree. The few trees we have compared known age history to the age in the charts have come out pretty close.

Tree Growth Factors by Species

tree species	growth factor	tree species	growth factor
Green Ash	4.0	Red Maple	4.5
White Ash	5.0	Norway Maple	4.5
Aspen spp	2.0	Silver Maple	3.0
American Beech	6.0	Sugar Maple	5.5
European Beech	4.0	Pin Oak	3.0
Basswood	3.0	Northern Red Oak	4.0
European White Birch	5.0	Scarlet Oak	4.0
River Birch	3.5	Shingle Oak	6.0
Paper Birch (aka White)	5.0	Shumark Oak	3.0
Yellow Buckeye	5.0	White Oak	5.0
Black Cherry	5.0	Bradford Pear	3.0
Kentucky Coffeetree	3.0	Austrian Pine	4.5
Cottonwood	2.0	Red Pine	5.5
Dogwood	7.0	Scotch Pine	3.5
American Elm	4.0	White Pine	5.0
Douglas Fir	5.0	Tulip Poplar (Tuliptree)	3.0
White Fir	7.5	Redbud	7.0
Shagbark Hickory	7.5	Colorado Blue Spruce	4.5
Common Horsechestnut	8.0	Norway Spruce	5.0
Ironwood	7.0	Sweetgum	4.0
Littleleaf Linden	3.0	American Sycamore	4.0
Black Maple	5.0	Black Walnut	4.5

Instructions

1. Determine the species of your tree.
2. With a tape measure, measure the circumference of your tree (in inches) 4 1/2 feet from the ground (breast height).
3. Determine the diameter of your tree at breast height (DBH) using the following formula:

Diameter = Circumference divided by 3.14 (pi)

4. Calculate the age of your tree using the table above and the following formula:

Age = Diameter x Growth Factor

The Tamarack Story

Tamarack trees are known for their beauty in the wild or as a landscape tree and for their use as knees in boatbuilding. The tree grows in cold, northern swamps, making it easier to pull the large roots from the loose soil once the tree is cut. Over history, some loggers and sawyers made extra money by getting these stumps out of the swamps and sawn into knees that were used in boats large and small. They are called knees because the wood used comes from the junction of the trunk and root, or trunk and branch, of a tree and is shaped like a bent knee. The grain would follow the curves needed for ribs or stems in guideboats and canoes and ceiling supports on large ships. Many of the small boats made by Old Town Canoe Co. before the 1950s had hackmatack, as it's called in Maine, for the transom and seat knees. The wood is fairly light and smooth to the touch and has a nice blond color. It is also full of resin, which makes it very long lasting. It also holds fastening well.

There was a record of a tamarack in NH that was close to the measurements of the national champion for that species. It had not been located or measured for many years, so the current Coos County forester, the recently retired Coos forester, and I searched a vast swamp area off of Bog Brook near the Androscoggin River to see if we could find it. After much traipsing around following moose trails in the knee-deep wet bog, we found several larger standing dead tamaracks (American larch) and decided it was likely one of those. On the way out, we found a smaller one and declared it the new county champion for that species, but it was not close to the size of the national champion.

A year or so later, Karen Zale from Vermont contacted me about restoring her father's canoe. She mentioned that its name was *Tamarack*. I got back to her and let her know that I would be able to do the work on the canoe and thought it was interesting that they named the canoe tamarack as I had been searching for a large tree of that type in NH. A long return email came back about how they had used the canoe when children and how her father had loved the tamarack tree. She had also attached a story of her father, John Zale, who as a WWII POW had survived the Bataan Death March when imprisoned in the Philippines and was aboard the "Ships of Hell" that transported them to another prison camp. While enroute Allied battleships had fired upon and sunk some of the enemy ships not knowing the prisoners were on board. Conditions were very bad during that journey, but Zale survived it and the following three years of harsh treatment at the POW camp. After the war, he came back to Vermont and became a scout leader who taught the scouts the art of survival and was widely respected among them.

Karen was trying to raise the money to restore the canoe, so I said I would start it off by knocking off some of the cost to do the work. She then contacted some of the former scouts who are now prominent businessmen and civic leaders. Without hesitation, they came up with the rest of the funds, and I was able to restore the canoe to its former glory. The decks of the canoe turned out to be made of tamarack and that name was repainted on the sides along with his POW #. It is now hanging in a scout lodge in Buffalo, NY. Karen put out a book later called *The Will to Survive* that tells the story of her father's life.

Not long after that, while leading a walk in Tamworth to see the largest pines in NH, a woman let us know that she had a large tamarack on her property that we should measure. It did not take much convincing to get us over there and we measured her tree. It turned out to be 6 points lower than the national champion. At the time, trees within 5 points of each other were considered a tie. Needless to say, we took a few more measuring trips to that tree but could never come up with that additional point to make it a national champ.

We submitted it to national as a competitor and low and behold the following year the other champion tree had died and the NH tree was the national champ. We were quite happy with the designation, even though it was short-lived because a larger tree was listed in Wisconsin the following year. The NH Big Tree Program has a saying "once a champion always a champion." Then again, in 2022 the Wisconsin tree must have died, because the NH tamarack is listed as national champion again. So, the tamarack has a special place in my mind as a significant type of tree in the Northeast, and this story shows how connections with people and trees live on in many different ways.

This tree is on private property and not available to view but the measurements are 118" C and 82' tall. Another noteworthy tamarack is available to visit in Effingham.

Tamarack *[Larix laricina]*

It's a pleasure to come across a grove of younger tamarack while hiking the northern woods. The needles can be bright green in the spring and golden yellow in the fall. If you look closely in the spring at the cones you will likely see small flowers where the new cones are starting. The bark has a unique look, as it's broken into many small, reddish-brown scales that make it look similar to some spruce types. Larger trees are not as good looking because they regularly have many dead lower branches and those pleasing needles and flowers are way up top and out of sight. At many times of the year, you will think the tree is dead. This is one of the few conifers that loses its needles in the winter and becomes completely bare.

My journeys to find tamarack in the woods most often bring me to

Tamarack.

Wilkinson Brook.

the wilder and wetter parts of the forest where you will see different trees such as black spruce and maybe some pitch pine or white cedar. The tamarack's other names include hackmatack and eastern larch. As lumber, it is a resinous wood that makes it durable in contact with the soil or water, a characteristic that makes boatbuilders seek it out for use in their crafts. It can also be used for posts and poles set in the ground. The wood has a slight orange tinge, and I have used knees from the curved root and trunk slabs to make stems for lapstrake boats and canoes. It's pleasing to work as you can chisel out rabbets easily and it feels smooth when planed to a fine finish. Linseed oil and varnish is added to take on the same sheen that you may see in the live tree with its fall needles glowing in the sunlight.

In the Pine River State Forest, this tree is unique for where it is situated in this part of the state, getting near the southern edge of its range. The lakes nearby have crystal-clear water with that fine, white sand showing throughout, making the land around them sought after for summer camps. This sand is perfect for growing pine trees and after the fires that went through here in the 1940s, the red pine and pitch pine have become prevalent. The 3,244-acre state forest is managed with frequent cuttings, giving some of the forest an open park like appearance.

Pine River flows through much of the flat land here, and several brooks feed into it. There are areas around the brooks that hold other types of conifers and give a special feel to this state park.

Wilkinson Brook comes off Green Mountain in Effingham, then flows through the state forest before it empties into the Pine River. I stopped briefly at the entrance to the state forest where the brook is dammed creating Hutchins Pond, and it looks like a great place to explore further. The best way to see the tamarack is to drive to Wilkinson Swamp Road and park in the pullover just shy of the bridge over Wilkinson Brook. Walk down the snowmobile trail to a small brook crossing and go east to find the tree. It's about 200 feet from the trail.

Keep a lookout for the tree with the spruce-like bark, as it is easy to miss. The needles are not really visible so ID it by its bark and dead lower branches. While not quite the size of our former national champion that is on the edge of an opening by a house, this is third-largest in the state and is much more pleasurable to visit in the woods of NH.

Difficulty rating 1   May need GPS.

83.5" CBH   85' VH   34 ACS'   Total Points 177   Fair Condition
GPS: N 43.715670°   W 071.039190°

Directions

In Ossipee, take a right going east on Granite Road for 1.7 miles and go left onto Effingham Road. After just under 1 mile, go right onto Clough Road and go 1.8 miles to a left onto Wilkinson Swamp Road. Go 0.3 miles to a small pullover area and park. You have gone too far if you go over the brook.

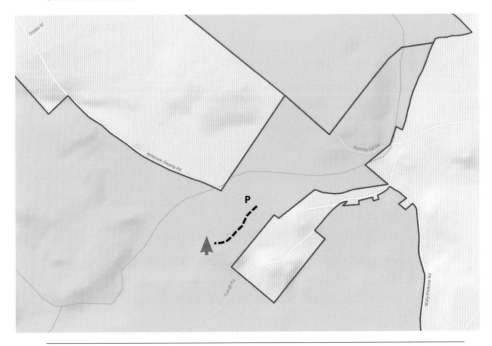

Franconia Notch

T he Franconia Notch State Park is a special place in the NH White Mountains with the highway and the headwaters of the Pemigewasset River both going through this high mountain pass. The Kinsman and Franconia mountain ranges loom over you on each side as you drive through with the eastern cliffs of Cannon Mountain appearing to crumble down into the pass. Lots of unique natural features draw great crowds in the summer and the fall. Hikers flock to the trails leading through the park and into the bordering White Mountains National Forest. Tourists pass through the notch for quick stops to see natural features and for the fall leaf peeping. The Flume can be seen near the beginning, with Echo Lake and the ski slopes of Cannon Mountain near the end. It's an amazing place where you can find all kinds of outdoor activities including Big Tree Hunting.

The trees to see here are yellow birch and red spruce, with many large birches scattered along both the Franconia Notch Recreation Trail and the Pemigewasset River foot trail. Both follow the river with the bike and rec trail mainly on the east side and the foot trail on the west side of the river. Start your walk or bike at the parking area for the Basin and take the trail by walking up on the rec trail and back down on the foot trail. Slopes are slight, so you could go either way on both. Another way

Franconia Notch.

Birch in October. ▶

Late October at the Notch from Lafayette campground.

to take the trip would be to take a bike on the rec trail and then lock it up at the Lafayette Campground and walk the other trail back to your vehicle and pick up the bike after. For mostly downhill on your bike, you could start at Lafayette Campground then leave your bike at the Basin and hike the trail back up. I started at the main parking area at the Flume Visitors Center for a longer ride on one visit.

After checking out The Basin, a glacial pothole in the rocks carved smooth by the swirling current of the river, head north on the trail and keep a look out for the trees. If on the rec trail, the big yellow birches will soon show up and have you peering into the woods to see more. There are many in the 100"–132"-circumference range. You can see one right on the bike trail that is 111" in circumference and 80' tall. Some of the biggest have lost their tops, but others seem to have good height on them. My take on these trees are that the area was cut of all the spruce growing here back in the late 1800s and then the birches grew in. The notch area was preserved by the state and the trees along the river trails and tourist spots were allowed to grow. While these birches are large and fairly old, at a likely age of about 150 years, I would not consider them old growth. With the abundance of large birches, I would hope those in charge of caring for the land here will keep them growing to end up as very grand trees. Yes, some are at the end of their life span, but those big old survivors would be special indeed.

You likely will be unable to avoid getting your feet hung up on the small shrubs that are abundant in the cool streamside woods under the birch canopies. This type of viburnum is called hobble bush for good reason, so watch your step to be sure you're not hobbling when leaving the trees. They are associated with the yellow birches in many areas.

Some of the nicknames include Witch-Hobble, Tangle-legs and Moose-wood. Wildlife that use this type of woods include the gray fox, fisher cats, and flying squirrels. Scarlet tanagers pass through southern NH in the early summer and end up breeding in these northern woods. Northern goshawks also prefer these woods.

You will also notice some large hemlocks and pines near the basin, along with the red spruce here and there. One red spruce in particular is worthy of your attention. This is growing on the side of the river bank right next to the Pemigewasset foot trail. In a great spot and easy to view, this is tied with another for state champion. Still sought after for their lumber value, the red spruce was once the most abundant tree on these mountainsides. You can still find pure stands of old trees in the higher elevations of Maine and NH.

Difficulty Rating 1

Yellow Birch

134" CBH   70' VH   46' ACS   Total Points 215   Fair Condition
GPS: N 44.133130°   W 071.683660°
∆ Grafton County Champion

Red Spruce

93" CBH   94' VH   29' ACS   Total Points 194   Excellent Condition
GPS: N 44.124500°   W 071.688650°
∆ State Champion; tied with 2 others.

Directions

Take I-93 to the White Mountain National Forest and Franconia State Park. On the Parkway look for a sign and exit to The Basin and get off there to the parking area.

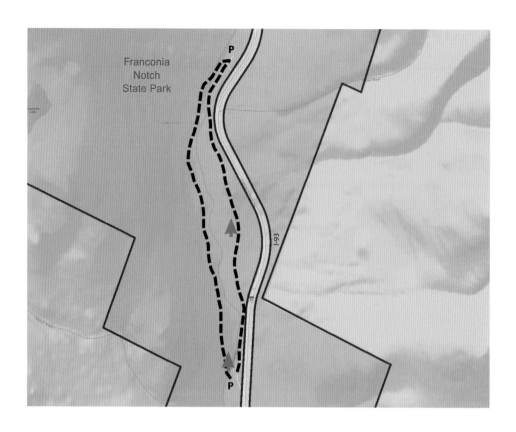

Quaking Aspen *[Populus tremuloides]*

T o visit this tree, you must go to the bottom of a one-time glacial lake bed by following a section of the Presidential Rail Trail that goes through the town of Jefferson and into the town of Whitefield. Starting from 115A, the trail is about 2.4 miles to Cherry Pond and 3.9 miles overall to the end on Hazen Road in Whitefield. The national champion white spruce can be seen near the other end and you may want to visit it also. It's a pretty long walk there and back at 7.8 miles, so you could visit the trees by driving to both ends and walking in about 0.7 mile for the aspen and 0.3 for the spruce. A better way is to bring your bike and ride the whole trail there and back while taking in the majestic views of the valley and mountain ranges hovering over it.

The public land here is held and managed as part of the Silvio O. Conte National Fish and Wildlife Refuge, with the Pondicherry Wildlife Preserve section around Cherry Ponds managed by NH Audubon.

Quaking aspen is another of the poplar type of tree that grows in colder climates and will rapidly take over newly cut or burned-over areas

Ancient lake bed.

Aspen.

to give the land a start for a new forest. It's not a very long-lived species though, and after one hundred years or so they will be gone for the most part, with a few hold-over larger standouts like this one left for a while. Wildlife loves the buds and seeds and will move right in along with the trees. It does not grow as large as big tooth aspen and the teeth on the leaves are smaller. As its name implies, it does quake a bit more. I read that the flat leaf stalks allow the leaves to tremble on this and some of the other species of poplar.

This tree ties as state champion with two others that happen to be in the same part of NH, with one of them also in Jefferson. One was national champion briefly and they all will compete for that status if the current national champion dies, which will likely happen soon.

To see a former national champion, check out the white spruce near the other end of the trail. The white spruce is a more northern tree and in northern New England it starts showing up above the mountains in Maine, New Hampshire, and Vermont, up to the Canadian border, and beyond. Used mostly for pulp in this country, it can be used for dimensional lumber and would be mixed in with the other spruces at your building supply yard. Sometimes I have noticed a smell like cat urine while sawing spruce in my shop and think it was when I used white spruce, as it is also called cat spruce.

This is a great example of the species and easy to see just over a wire fence about 60' off the rail trail. It has many dead branches from the ground level up showing that it must have been open-grown for some time.

Difficulty Rating 2

Quaking Aspen

96" CBH   81' VH   42' ACS   Total Points 187   Fair Condition
GPS: N 44.36873°   W 071.48797°
Δ Tied for State Champion

White Spruce

105" CBH 96' VH 41' ACS   Total Points 211   Excellent Condition
GPS: N 44.360869° W 071.533753°
Δ State Champion

Directions

From Route 2 in Jefferson, take 115 just over 3 miles and take a right onto 115A and go 0.3 of a mile to the parking for the Presidential Rail Trail.

New Hampshire White Pines *[Pinus strobus]*

New Hampshire has some important history associated with the eastern white pine as this tree was a resource sought after by the colonists and the British, with laws made about its cutting playing a large part in driving the American Revolution. The virgin trees grew in abundance along the large rivers, where they were cut and floated downstream or to mills created along the many smaller streams so the logs could be sawn.

We can see some trees of that size in a few areas where the older forests have been preserved. Those shown here are in the White Mountain region for the most part, with one in the lower SW part of the state. In Sharon, there is an enjoyable trip along Meadow Brook to a great, straight tall pine. Travel up to the mountains to the Big Pines Trail in Waterville Valley, an out of the way ski resort with hiking trails into the National Forest. On the Kancamagus Highway, you can see three or four large pines and learn about the history of the King's Broad Arrow mark, Then paddle across Chocorua Lake to one of the largest in the state before heading to nearby Hemenway State Forest for a real old-growth treat and the northern New England champion for that species.

Waterville Valley pines.

Meadow Brook Pine

One of the best-formed eastern white pines in northern New England is found on the outskirts of this brook in the small town of Sharon, NH. It's in the Robert P. Bass Memorial Forest, named after the state's fifty-third governor, elected in 1910. He was also a farmer and forestry expert who served for a time as chairman of the state forestry commission. His grandson is Charlie Bass, who served as a US Congressman in more recent times. This 885-acre town forest is a great asset to the town and is an important deer wintering area, with some pockets of old-growth trees noted in its natural resources report.

I was told it was best to access the tree from Jarmany Hill Road, but to make a more interesting hike to the tree, I started by parking on the side of the road by the former arts center in a pullover at the start of the trail on Route 123. A woods road goes behind the center with a trail arrow that sends you to the right, down a newly blazed trail following yellow ribbons on the trees. This trail crosses Meadow Brook a few times on step stones which can be tricky in winter or high water. After following it for some time past an old stone bridge foundation, the trail seemed to just die out on the other side of the stream. The town has since improved the trail and added markers, so you can find your way easier from across the brook and over to the pine. On a more recent trip, Ken Callahan, who made the stone crossings and helps care for the trails, showed the way. After the last brook crossing, he pointed out some hemlock trunks that were blown down by the hurricane of 1938 and are laying near the trail all pointing in the same direction. When you come to the junction of the Big Tree Trail go left following the yellow markers a short distance to the tree. A brochure with a trail map is available through the Sharon Conservation Commission.

For just an in-and-out hike from Jarmany Hill Road, there is a small pullover that fits a car or two in the summer where you can park, but it's not plowed in the winter. A trail goes in there through some heavy growth of young saplings, and then you should see a stonewall. Yellow trail ribbons show you the path, with a wide woods tote road much of the way, which then narrows to a nice trail mostly downhill past a stone wall junction and continuing to the tree.

You can't miss the tree from that trail. It stands out with its chunky bark and straight, tall trunk that goes up 120' in the air. Surely it could have been a mast pine for the King's Navy.

Difficulty rating 3 Stream crossings.

157" CBH   120' VH   45' ACS   Total Points 288   Excellent Condition
GPS: N 42.81703°   W 071.93108°

Directions

From Route 101 in Peterborough, take Route 123 south for 3.8 miles and just past the town offices on the left you will see the parking area for the former Sharon Arts Center on the right. Do not park there. Just beyond the buildings there is a small pullover next to a triangular stone wall on the side of the road where the trail starts. You can park there and start the hike. If you want to hike in from the other trail, go about 1.5 miles further on 123 and go right or west on Jarmany Hill Road. After about a mile, start looking for the small pullover on the right.

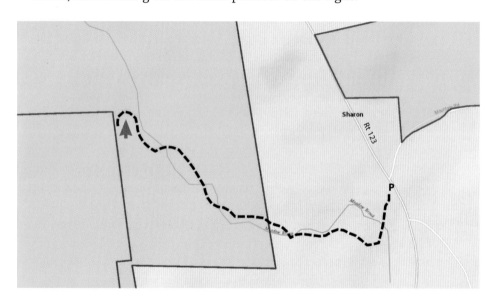

Big Pines Trail – Waterville Valley

I have lived in NH all my life but for some reason never visited Waterville Valley. I guess it's because I don't downhill ski and always passed by the access road on my way to the Whites. Now that I've been there, I'm sure to go back. To get to there, you go on an over-ten-mile-long road passing through the national forest that ends at the small town nestled in the mountain valley. It has a town-square of restaurants and stores with the remainder mostly inns, condos, mountains, and the Mad River. Lots of things going on when I visited on a long weekend, with downhill skiing,

Big Pines trail sign.

hockey tournaments, and many other events on the calendar. You could start visiting trees here with an easy walk on the Tyler's Spring Trail. From the town square, walk across the dam by the pond and turn right on the Village X-C Ski Trail, then right on a bridge over Snows Brook. Tyler's Spring Trail goes off to the right just before another bridge, this one over the Mad River. It's a short walk to the large pine next to the river. Although this pine is close in size to the ones on the Big Pines Trail, it was not as impressive looking. Worth a visit just for the walk and to compare with the other pines outside of town.

Those pines require that you pay the $5 fee in the Livermore Road parking area and follow the Livermore Road toward the Greely Ponds Trail. The road is closed to vehicles in the winter and groomed for cross-country skiing. Skis might be the way to go, but the trail off Livermore to the pines has a pretty steep section that may be hard to get up and down on skis. Snowshoeing is probably the best way to go, just be sure to stay off the groomed ski trail on Livermore Road. I was able to walk with my winter boots on the well-packed trail on the road. After going by the Mad River and the trail to Greeley Ponds, go up the hill a bit and you will see the Big Pines trail on the left. Don your snowshoes and head into the narrow trail. It's a close-feeling trail with balsam fir all around you for the most part. It's not marked, so I thought I lost track of the trail until I realized it went down the fairly steep slope toward the river. In the snow, it's hard to see what's under you, so be careful here. It's not as bad as I imagined going back, but I did have to use my hands to work my way up. Once at the bottom, go a short distance to another small drop and the trees will be right in front of you. They certainly draw your attention with the long, clear trunks and somewhat old look to the bark. Not the biggest for their type, but with three together and another a short way off they will impress, and the river is right nearby, adding to the appeal of the trip.

Not sure why these pines were left when this whole valley was cut over in the late 1800s. Maybe they were used in some way to help hold logs that were run down the river. Maybe they were at a site that the loggers liked so they left them. Maybe there was some connection that locals had to them at the time. My guess is as good as yours. The forest around them looks much younger, so logging must have gone on here in the 1900s also. The pines are still here though, and it makes a great hike to go see them.

Difficulty Rating 3

Tyler's Spring Trail Pine

134" CBH   109' VH   48' ACS   Total Points 255   Good Condition
GPS: N 43.951468° W 071.511859° Might be off. Tree is next to the river on the trail.

Biggest Pine on Big Pines Trail

134" CBH   116' VH   34' ACS   Total Points 258   Good Condition
GPS: N 43.97142°   W 071.50463°

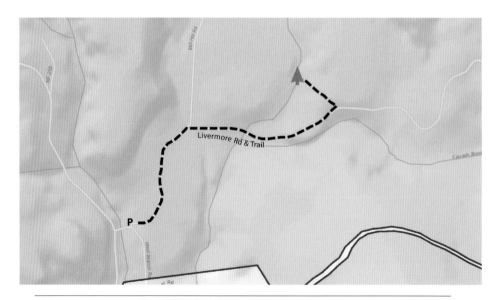

Directions

From I-93 in Campton, take Route 49 to Waterville Valley. Stay on 49, which is the main road that goes through the town. After Village Road, the entrance to the central village, take a right when rounding the corner staying on 49 North. Go past the golf course and tennis courts, then take a left onto West Branch Road. In 0.7 miles, turn into the Livermore Trails parking area.

King's Pines

Over the years, I have heard several people tell about eastern white pine trees that are survivors of the trees that were marked with the King's Broad Arrow mark. The story of King's Pines begins with the fact that the great English, Spanish, and Dutch armadas of merchant and war ships required large, straight trees to use for the masts and bowsprits of these fleets. A supply of scotch pines and other types that was coming from the Baltic area in Europe and Russia was depleted by the early 1600s, and the shipbuilders had to piece together the masts. The English started looking to their colonized land in New England. We had the great, large pines that were forest-grown close together, causing them to obtain great heights and have trunks clear of knots for some distance. By the 1650s, mast ships were sent over to transport the great logs back to England so they could fit them out in the boats of the Royal Navy.

The colonists were also using the pine for their houses and furniture. The large, long logs were cut into boards and the admiralty decided measures should be taken to preserve the trees for their use as masts. The woods in what is now Massachusetts, Maine, and New Hampshire were surveyed and trees within ten miles of the navigable waterways that met the needs of a mast were marked with the King's Broad Arrow mark, a three-legged arrow mark cut into the trunk. Colonists who cut the trees were subject to a one-hundred-pound fine. The lumber was much more valuable sawn into boards than the bounty paid, so although the fine was levied on those who cut trees of the large size even without the king's mark, or on boards at sawmills over 24" wide, the large mast trees kept disappearing. Several skirmishes between the king's agents and the locals occurred. The Broad Arrow policy was a contributing factor for the colonial uprising and start of the American Revolution.

When cut for masts, the felling of the tree was carefully carried out to preserve the logs. A bed of other trees was first cut to cushion the mast tree to prevent it from shattering on the bare ground. It had to be felled in the correct direction so the great log could be hauled out by a team of oxen. Cut with an ax, it took two men, one on each side, to bring the huge tree crashing to the ground. The tree was chopped to length at the highest point of sound wood of the correct diameter and the limbs cut off.

Care was taken to keep the bark on throughout the process and to keep the resin in the wood "wet," as the resin provided the suppleness and flexibility required for a good mast. Hauled out in the winter, a road was prepared and often wet down so it would ice over for a smooth haul. These skid paths are still named "Mast Road" in many northern New England towns. Wherever the turns were made during the trip to the sea, the oxen and log required a large cleared area for the turn radius. This was often near the center of a settlement and those spots became the "greens" in many of the new towns and are still there today. Once at the ports where they were shipped out, the bark was taken off and the logs were stored in the tidewater until they could be loaded into the hold of the mast ships.

Trees of the size required for masts of 3' in diameter and 120' long can still be seen. A great spot where several are growing in close proximity is off the Rail and River Trail behind the Russell Colbath House on the Kancamagus Highway. The highway itself is an adventure, with many stops and hiking trails as you travel through the White Mountain National Forest from Conway to Lincoln. As a child, the hairpin turns most exited me while driving the route with my family. From the parking area, walk toward the barn and find the trailhead. The short loop trail will bring you to the river, and the trees are near the sign describing the mast pines. We measured three and they all were over 11' in circumference and 120' tall.

Even on the trip made here, we stopped at a tractor dealership where a worker there said he used to do some logging and knew of a marked King's Pine in nearby Chatham on property he had logged years ago. The tree was marked to be preserved by the forest manager at the time. Turns out it the manager retired and the we did not get more info. I asked at the Saco Ranger Station and the foresters who managed land in that area knew nothing of it. This is the case with other King's Pines that I have followed up on. Information is lacking on exactly where the tree is, or the original contact person is hard to reach or does not reply. While it is possible that some trees like these here were large enough in

1700 and could be considered King's Pines, most foresters will tell you that it is highly unlikely that the tell-tale King's Broad Arrow mark will be distinguishable after two centuries.

Difficulty Rating 1

Biggest Pine

142" CBH   122' VH   43' ACS   Total points   275   Excellent Condition
GPS: N 43.99688°   W 071.33916°

Directions

From Route 16 in Conway, take the Kancamagus Highway about halfway to Lincoln. Look for the parking area for the Russell Colbath House and park there. If you go in the winter, the snow in the parking area will likely not be plowed. If that is the case, you can park on the side of the road as long as all four tires are off the tarred road. You might need a shovel. Don't block any gates.

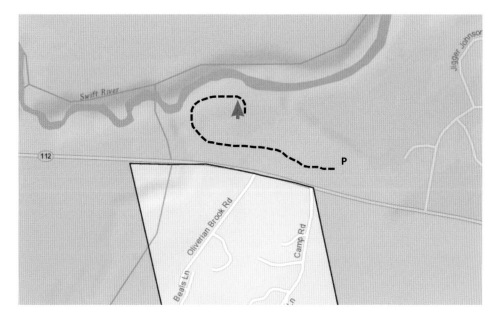

Chocorua Lake Pine

Some of the most iconic photos in NH are taken from the bridge next to this lake. The view of Mount Chocorua with its unmistakable peak hovering over the water draws photographers from near and far. It's right

Chocorua pine.

next to Route 16, and that view prepares you for your visit to this side of the White Mountains and the grand vistas as you travel through them. The mountain is in the national forest, and much of the land around this lake is conserved by other groups, offering many trails to hike near the lake, nearby ponds, and mountainside. The Frank Bolles Nature Preserve is owned by the Nature Conservancy and co-managed by the

Chocorua Lake Conservancy. The Nature Conservancy owns over thirty properties in NH. Most have special natural features that their members deem important to protect. This land includes kettle ponds, swamps, lake frontage, and a huge pine tree.

There are many large pines in this part of the state, with Hemenway Forest nearby and some private lands with similar sized trees. I believe some searching may yield a few more outstanding pines reaching to great heights. To see this one, head out from the parking spot on Bolles Road and cross the wet stream to catch the trail that goes up near a clearing and house on the left. You then come to a sign for the Heron Pond Trail and head toward that. You will soon pass a large wooden sign showing that you are entering the Frank Bolles Preserve and head to the next junction at 0.6 of a mile from the parking area. Take a right to follow Lake Trail down a small hill and start looking for the pine on your left. This pine may have been a boundary tree, as it's close to the preserve's edge. There is a house nearby, so be respectful of the neighbors while here. The trail continues a short distance down to the lake, so you may want to take in the view there. Another way to visit this tree is by canoe. You can put in near the bridge next to Route 16 and paddle across the lake then catch the Lake Trail to the tree. The banking is a few feet high and you will have to tie up the canoe to a tree and scramble over the bank. GPS coordinates are given to the landing in directions to the tree.

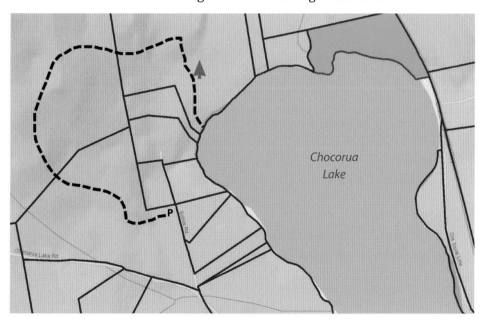

Difficulty Rating 2

164" CBH   126' VH   43' ACS   Total Points 300   Good Condition
GPS: N 43.907883°   W 071.246943°

Directions

From Route 16 in Tamworth, take the left onto Chocorua Lake Road just before the lake when coming from the south. Follow the dirt road for about 1 mile and then take a right at the fork onto Bolles Road. Go about a quarter mile to the end and you'll find spaces for two or three cars at the sign for the Bolles Preserve parking on the left.

If canoeing to the tree, park at the beginning of Chocorua Lake road and paddle across the small lake to the coordinates N 43.906205° W 071.245759°. Leave the canoe tied to a tree and climb over the two- or three-foot banking and find the Lake Trail with a sign for the preserve. Go up the trail about 700 feet to the tree on the right.

Big Pines Natural Area and Great Hill

This is about the best forest of large pines and hemlocks I have visited in northern New England. I would guess there are close to one hundred Big Tree-sized pines over 3' in diameter, with many over 120" in circumference and the state's largest single stem pine located here. It's a great hike, too, in the outskirts of the White Mountain National Forest in the Hemenway State Forest along trails maintained by the Tamworth Conservation Commission. Coming out of Tamworth 113A or the Chinook Highway named for the sled dog training kennels that were once located in the area, the winding road goes through dense woods along the Swift River. You will see a pullover by the sign saying Big Pines Natural Area inviting you to stop for a visit. The trail starts into the woods and the mailbox might have maps in it. Grab one if available then continue over the bridge to a sign showing the main loop trail with a spur trail up to the Great Hill Tower.

Take a left on the loop trail along the edge of the river and along the fairly steep slope a while until it flattens out. As you start looping right, you will see some impressive pines right off. These were the results of the last logging operation some time ago and have been saved for your viewing pleasure. I measured the circumference of a few at 140". You will continue to see these all along the trail. When you come to the spur trail you can take that toward the fire tower. The forest starts to change, with a deeper, darker woods look as eastern hemlocks start making an appearance.

With thirty or so big and old-looking trees, the hemlocks are as impressive as the pines. Several are very stately looking, and the largest is among the top three or four in the state.

Continuing up the spur trail, it gets steeper and you may want to rest against some of these old friends as you go along. Soon they get scarcer, and you will have to concentrate on getting to the top of a fairly good climb. After resting, a trip to the top of the fire tower will reward you with views of the nearby mountains, including Chocorua and the small town of Tamworth in its deep woods setting.

The trail down is much easier, and after reviewing all those hemlocks, take a left back onto the loop trail then continue down till you see the biggest single stem pine in the state. This is the tallest officially measured tree in NH. Its base of large roots come off the ground and holds the straight trunk as it rises and rises until it reaches 150 feet in height. Be careful around the base and try not to scramble on it too much, as it may be getting too much foot traffic by this well-traveled trail. It had been measured many times and some have actually climbed it for precise height measuring. Records back about fifteen years or so show that the measurements have stayed about the same, making me wonder if its time in this world is nearing an end.

When ready, head back down but keep a lookout for turn toward a small stream that the trail crosses, as it's easy to miss. Follow the trail toward the river and parking where you started. I guarantee you will have enjoyed your visit.

Difficulty Rating 3–4   Steep areas. No off trail required.

Hemlock

138" CBH   110' VH   Did not get ACS.   Good Condition
GPS: N 43.879650°   W 071.296500°

White Pine

179" CBH   150' VH   47' ACS   Total Points 341   Good Condition
GPS: N 43.884112°   W 071.295290°
Δ State champion

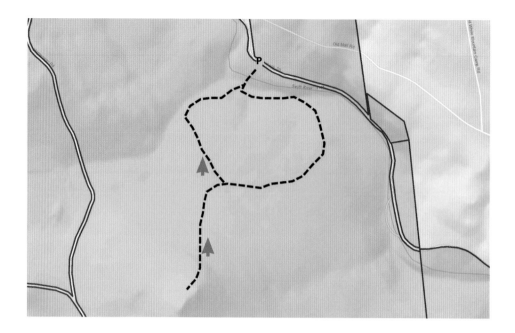

Directions

From Route 16, take a left onto Depot Road and follow just over 3 miles to the end. Turn right on 113 and go 0.8 miles to the center of Tamworth and stay straight on 113A, the Chinook Highway, just over 2.5 miles to the parking area on the left.

Vermont

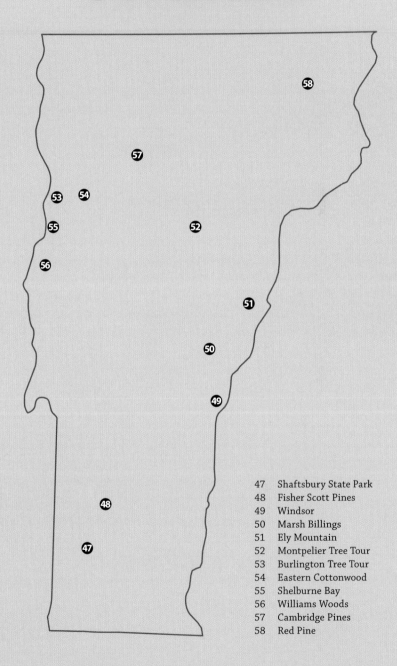

Shaftsbury State Park

T his park in the southwest part of the state is an invigorating place to visit, with its outstanding swimming beach and the Vermont mountain scenery all around you. It has several outbuildings, one of which is providing the area forester with a home right on the property. Within sight of the forester's home is the former state champion Scotch pine. This tree has the largest circumference for this type in Vermont, is the best looking for its type, and is in the best setting.

To see the tree, all that is required is a short walk from the parking area to the beach. To make a hike out of it, you can take the trail around the lake. The trail brings you along an esker to the former small mill pond and then through the woods and back to the beach area where if you look around you may see foundations and other signs of the land's former use. The wildlife I associate with this spot are the sandpipers that I saw skimming across the top of the lake in mid-April. They like the same white sand that the pines thrive in. I could also hear geese calling from their nesting area in the wetlands in the outlet just past the dam.

At one time, water from a meadow in the area was bottled and sold as mineral water for healing purposes. Known then as Vermont Healing Springs, the meadow was later flooded to run a small sawmill. Still later, in the early 1900s, a concrete dam was built to create the lake we see now. An inn and bungalows for a summer colony was established, and then it became Camp Avalon, a girl's summer camp. In the 1920s, the cabins were rented out to visitors and a campground was set up. Electricity was provided by the dam and water from the healing springs was pumped in to the site.

The John James family owned and ran the campground and maintained the cottages. They also planted the Scotch pine and Norway spruce that you see here now. The state of Vermont purchased the property of 84 acres in 1974 and created Shaftsbury State Park. You can still rent out a cabin here and at some other Vermont sites owned by the state. The property is enjoyed by many people all year and I am sure that you will feel invigorated after your visit, if not a result of the mineral water, then definitely by the scotch pine and mountain views from the lakeshore.

◀ *Scotch pine.*

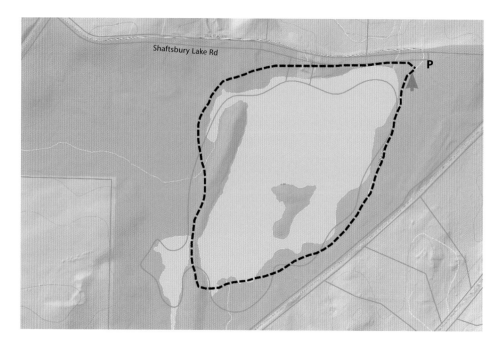

Difficulty Rating 2 If going around the lake.

111" CBH   80' VH   56' ACS   Total Points 205   Good Condition
GPS: N 42.02112°   W 073.17898°

Δ State Champion

Directions

From Bennington, take Route 7A a little over 9 miles to Shaftsbury and Shaftsbury Lake Road on the right. Go to the state park beach at the end of the road.

Fisher-Scott Memorial Pines

This twenty-two-acre eastern white pine forest in Arlington holds some of Vermont's most impressive trees for the type, known not mainly for their girth but more so for their height. The gulley with Mill Brook has pines growing along the hillsides on both sides, all competing with those further up on the hill. The resulting race to the sunlight makes for very tall trees, and I have heard some measure 160' in this area. Recent storms caused much damage, and you will notice the tops taken right off some pines and others that are snapped in half near the bottom.

This forest dedicated to John Redwood Fisher; his wife, the educator and novelist, Dorothy Canfield Fisher; their son, James Canfield Fisher

Retired and current Bennington County foresters Jim White (left) and Cory Creagan.

or "Doc Jimmy"; and grandson, John Scott Jr. Doc Jimmy had volunteered with a group of US Army Rangers to go behind enemy lines in the Philippines to help rescue Allied prisoners from a POW camp and was killed in the process. A book called *The Ghost Soldiers* by Hampton Sides was written about the remarkable mission. A movie called *The Great Raid* was also produced.

Dorothy was one of the most popular novelists in the country in the early 1920s when she introduced the book *The Brimming Cup*. Education was Dorothy's other interest. She pushed to educate women and started the well-known Montessori teaching system for children. The family loved these woods and visited them often. Their daughter, Sally Fisher-Scott, donated the land to the state because of the family's appreciation of the great trees seen here. You will find a plaque in their honor along the trail near the top of the hill bordering the brook. The largest tree near the plaque looks to have been blown down several years ago, but there are many large-diameter pines with old-growth bark nearby that should impress you. The largest in circumference is near the blown-over trunk, while the tallest we measured is down on the steep slope near the brook. Not much of a hike, but you can wander among these old trees that likely started growing about three hundred years ago after a wind or fire event created a clearing for them. The steep slopes of the brook probably kept the trees from being cut when sheep and cattle were raised and much of the state was cleared in the 1800s. The park has the honor of being designated a National Natural Area for the pines' size and significance to the country.

Difficulty Rating 1–2 For slope to brook.

Pine 1

136" CBH   132" VH   30' ACS   Total Points 275   Good Condition
GPS: N 43.103732°   W 73.138942°

Brookside Pine

130" CBH   140' VH   38' ACS   Total Points 279   Good Condition
GPS: N 43.103787°   W 73.139950°

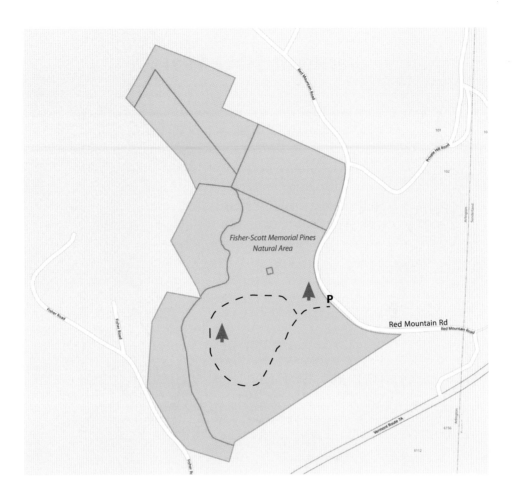

Directions

From Route 7A near the border of Sunderland and Arlington, take Red Mountain Road. Go about a ¼ mile uphill and look for a pullover on the left with a sign for the trail into the pines.

Vermont State Seal

The eastern white pine is so important to the state of Vermont that they included it in the state seal used to represent the state on all its important documents. The pine on the seal is said to have been drawn by a British soldier who was a currier for clandestine discussions with Canada just after the Revolutionary War while Vermont was deciding its future as a state. These discussions took place in Arlington, and the pine was growing on the hillside near the river where the currier would visit a girl he was courting. The drawing was engraved on an oxhorn drinking cup that Ira Allen, brother of the famed Revolutionary fighter Ethan Allen, took note of and decided to use a modified version of it when designing the state seal in 1777.

The tree was affected by pine weevils, which caused it to develop several trunks starting about 20' high, giving it an unusual look with its broad crown. Ira used that look and incorporated fourteen branches in the tree he designed, signifying the thirteen original colonies and the hope that Vermont would become the fourteenth. This original seal engraving, used for many years when stamping documents, eventually wore out and new seals were made that drastically changed the appearance of the pine tree in its center. In 1937, a new die for the seal was made that closely resembles the original seal, rediscovered a few years earlier. That year, with new

interest in the tree, the property the pine is on was purchased by the town of Arlington and the park was made around it.

The tree fell in 1978 when its rotted base gave away in a windstorm. The state and town decided to salvage as much of the tree as possible. Even though the main trunk was rotted, they got thirty-seven logs, yielding 6,500 board feet of lumber. Over the years, many pieces of furniture, signs, and plaques have been made from the wood. The park has been kept up, with a new pine that was planted from the seeds of the original, and you can still see the mound of the rotted stump and roots of that old tree. It looks like the newly planted pine has been trimmed to grow as multi-trunk, mimicking the original tree.

This historic site dedicated to a single eastern white pine will make a good stop to appreciate this type of tree's value to the state and region. Visit it while checking out the Fisher Scott Pines a few miles away.

Directions

From Route 7A in the center of Arlington, take Route 313 west about ¾ of a mile to the park with a small pullover on the right. It's a tight fit, but you can get the vehicle off the road. Watch for traffic that can be traveling somewhat fast here.

Windsor Tree Tour

This small town has a few areas that make it a worthwhile place for a tree tour. The history here is important to the state, being the earliest settlement in Vermont. The old homes and estates are associated with names such as William Maxwell Evarts, who served as US Senator for New York, US Attorney General, and US Secretary of State. There is an historic walking tour that features over forty houses. One, the Old Constitution House, was a tavern owned by Elijah West where delegates met in 1777 to write up the constitution for the newly formed Republic of Vermont. In 1791, Vermont was admitted to the Union as the fourteenth state. The state constitution was the first in the country to prohibit slavery and include the right to vote without property or income restrictions. It also became the first state to establish a system of public schools. The American Precision Museum is in the former Robbins and Lawrence Armory, where the American system of mass production was started. The factory-made rifles with interchangeable parts in a method that was widely copied by famous gun makers like Smith & Wesson and Winchester.

There are many other things to see while biking or walking through town. Check out the longest two-span covered bridge in the world, going over the Connecticut River. This used to connect the Cornish colony of

Bridge over the Connecticut River.

Hackberry.

artists on the NH side to Windsor and the train station. Be sure to walk your horses though! The famous sculptor Augustus Saint-Gaudens lived and worked in Cornish with other sculptors, artists, writers, etc. who visited from Boston and New York by taking a train to the station in Windsor. The American Precision Museum may be a good place to stop, or you can get some food at the farmers' market if you plan the right day. If not, visit one of the local restaurants. The town is also known for its artists and has supported the arts by providing shops in some of the historic buildings.

The best way to start seeing the trees is from behind the old homes on Route 5. Park in town in a small lot beside Rite Aid, then go to Maxwell Perkins Lane. Behind a maintenance building is a path into the small wooded area. You will notice an unusual-looking tree at the back corner of the building. This is a hackberry. Hackberry is native to southern New England and fingers of its growth range come up the Connecticut River Valley and along the Champlain Valley on the other side of the state. This

Mt. Ascutney over pumpkin field.

is about the extent of its range in Vermont, and although this relative of the elm is commonly planted in towns as street trees, these most likely have naturally grown. Their deep roots can go down twenty feet or more, so this spot near water is ideal for them. The small fruit is eaten by many bird species, including partridge, cedar waxwings, and robins, along with small mammals who gather them either in the tree or on the ground. People would mix the hackberries with corn and fat to make porridge or dried and crushed the fruit to add flavor to other foods. The lumber can be used for lighter-colored furniture where it is abundant but is most commonly used for firewood. I have never seen the wood or a tree in my part of NH, so have not tried to work with it. It is said to rot easily and was not used in boat work.

To find the largest hackberry in the state, you will have to work your way into the woods along the edge of the yard behind the parking lot for the building. The yard cleanup is dumped here, so there is no real trail in. There is also a lot of undergrowth and dead branches that you will have to make your way through. I promise it will be worth the effort. The tree has many cables and steel rods holding the branches together and even though a large dead branch is hanging by a cable above, these have likely helped keep the tree from splitting apart and losing more branches. It looks as though more help is needed. Notice the odd way the tree has attempted to seal the wounds around the rods by growing up the steel and the way the bark has curled up around the openings where branches have rotted off. On a more recent visit, some of the large branches had died.

Check out a few of the old-looking hemlocks and a pretty good cherry while here, then head out around the pond to Paradise. Paradise Park, that is. Go to the very edge of the yard behind the big linden tree to find a faint trail that goes past a back yard and tree house where, if you bear right, it goes down a slope through a backyard and then to a better trail that takes you around Lake Runnemede. Paradise Park was once part of the estate of the Evarts family, who put in carriage roads and dammed Hole Brook to create Lake Runnemede. The town purchase 115 acres from the Evarts in 1942, forming the Windsor Town Forest. Another 109 acres around the lake was added more recently to help protect the globally endangered Ogden's Pond Weed found here.

Trail maps are available, and if walking you can go around the lake and come out on the other side of town on Route 5. The pines are near a shelter and picnic area and along a steep hillside along the lake. They are another example of tall Vermont hillside pines, with some here reaching over 130' in height. If your bikes are at the parking area, you can make a loop walk and end up back at them. Ride back toward town and head over to the Ascutney Cemetery to check out a catalpa, oaks, and some more nice pine trees.

Go up the long driveway, made of steel gray stones, to the cemetery, then further on to middle of the cemetery, where you will see many fair-sized pines lining the road. A worker told me they lost one of the larger ones recently, but the largest left is still a pretty good tree at 128' tall and 141" circumference. There are also some good-sized oaks spread throughout.

Difficulty Rating 3   Some distance for round trip.

1. Hackberry

152" C   79' VH   57' ACS   Total Points   245   Poor Condition
GPS: N 43.448226°   W 072.38682°
Δ State Champion

2. Eastern White Pine near hut

137" CBH   128' VH   74' ACS   Total Points 283   Fair Condition
GPS: N 43.48519°   W 072.39485°

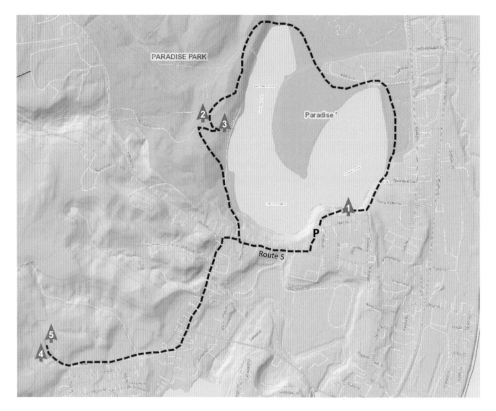

3. Pine on Zig Zag Trail hillside

130" CBH   139' VH   34' ACS   Total Points 277   Good Condition
GPS: N 43.485330° W 072.394850°

4. Catalpa

125" CBH   73' VH   59' ACS   Total Points 213   Good Condition
GPS: N 43.477380° W 072.401600°

5. Pine in cemetery

141" CBH   128' VH   55' ACS   Total Points 283   Good Condition
GPS: N 43.478126° W 072.402812°   May not be exact but in the area.

Directions

From I-91 heading south, take Exit 9 to Route 5 South to Windsor. Turn into the Rite Aid on the right at 3.5 miles. Park in the small lot on the side near the woods.

Marsh-Billings

This tour will bring you from the town of Woodstock with its elegant eighteenth-century homes in the hills that you see surrounding it. The forests behind some of these homes have been well managed for over one hundred years. You should start or end your trip with a walk through the town that is enjoyable any time of the year. There are many restaurants, a never-ending country store, the Marsh-Billings National Park, and other attractions that are sure to keep you busy.

Start looking at the trees by parking at the Marsh-Billings farm and walk to the mansion area. Near the old carriage house turned visitors center on the right is the state champ Norway spruce. Look for the biggest of many that surround the buildings here. The nearby hillsides also have many in a more forested setting. You cannot help but notice why

Norway spruce.

the Norway spruce is still sought-after as a landscape tree near homes. The long needles and drooping branches add a stylish and classy look that enhances the architecture of the buildings and the layout of the grounds.

George Perkins Marsh was from an influential family, and in the mid-1800s became a well-known naturalist across the US and in Europe. He was a scholar who read in twenty languages and traveled the world studying forestry and the effects unbridled use of natural resources had on the great civilizations in Egypt and Europe. Educated in nearby Dartmouth as a lawyer, he was very involved in forestry on his land in Woodstock. His book *Man and Nature* helped changed the direction of the country at a time when industrial expansion was the norm, with no concern for the environment. President Theodore Roosevelt was inspired by his book to go on and establish the US Forest Service.

Frederick Billings and his family eventually owned the farm and took on the task of following Marsh's writings by purchasing the surrounding land, which had been stripped bare of trees by fire and sheep farmers. They added plantings of larch, scotch pine, red pine, and Norway spruce to the estate, and you can see the results now with the tallest of some of these types of trees in the region.

From the Visitors Center, walk past the mansion and take the roadway that goes past the the Belvedere, a long white building, which houses a bowling alley and greenhouse with gardens surrounding it. Just beyond the building, there is a very large white pine on the left. This is the largest I measured on the grounds, with a few other pines, smaller in diameter but taller in height, mixed in with Norway spruce a hundred feet or so down the road. From there, go back up and get on Cemetery Road and head toward the Horse Shed. When arriving at a small clearing before the shed, you'll see a pine on the right that is very similar in size to the lower tree. Heading past another similar tree next to the shed, stay on Cemetery Road past Billings Trail, continuing to catch Upper Meadow Trail to Mountain Road.

On your way up the carriage road, notice the well-managed forest-land around you. The hardwoods are nicely thinned, allowing for good growth that can be harvested at some future date for lumber and fire-wood. Catch Summer Pasture Road near the top by bearing right along the edge of the pasture, then go right again to North Ridge Loop. Following the loop toward the Pogue, you will start seeing some old hemlocks close by. At the junction of the trail toward the Pogue Loop, you

Hemlock.

will see the largest hemlock that I measured. It's in fair shape with a hollow middle and a decent crown. Many of the hemlocks and pines seen on the property are likely left from when the forest was beginning to be managed by Billings. Now they are impressive, with many others just on the verge of reaching Big Tree size spread throughout the tops of the hills here.

I continued on past the Pogue and was going to check out the red pine loop but got sidetracked through some Norway maples and along the Mount Tom Road into the Larch Trail. A map is available that shows the dates these plots were planted. It says 1887 for the larch. In the more forested setting, they did not seem to get as large as many I have seen in cemeteries, but there are a few impressive ones next to the trail near the end. The good-sized white pines seen spread around as you get back to Mount Tom Road were planted in 1917. You can get an idea of what a one-hundred-year-old pine looks like. If you managed to look at the red pine grove further back, they were planted fairly recently in 1952.

Once you reach the end of Mount Tom Road at South Peak, take a good look at the views of Woodstock and the surrounding hills. From there, I took the Precipice Trail (no trail sign), which headed down from the last viewing area. At first, it's pretty steep, with posts and cables helping you go by the ledges, then it starts a large number of long switchbacks going down the mountain. I found them annoying in the distance you go while seeing the path right below you, but I'm sure they help runoff from ruining the trail, so try to stay on the trail and resist the urge to take a shortcut. Probably better to go up this way if starting out in town.

You will see some red oaks, which do not seem to live long on the mountain, and a few big pines near the bottom. As you come out to a sidewalk, bear right and there is a nice white ash near the kiosk in Faulkner Park. I headed out to River Street and across a covered bridge then into a farmers' market on the Greens with music playing, crafts, and foods for sale, making for a resounding end to the hike. The empanadas were great to fill up on. The market is there on Wednesdays if you want to plan for it. Otherwise, head into town and check out the local restaurant offerings.

As another part to this tree tour, if you want see the very tall Scotch and red pines, you can drive around to Prosper Road and take a short walk in to the trees, or you can make a hike of it by starting from the mansion and going across Mount Tom to the trees, a distance of about four miles round trip.

The Scotch pines and red pines can be easily seen from the trail. The state champions for these species were here, but a windstorm recently knocked them down. Maybe you can use a clinometer and find another champion here. You can tell you're in the Scotch pine areas by looking for the smooth, orange bark on the top half of this introduced species. The trees here are very tall from the hillside growth, with each one trying to reach up past the tree above it on the hill to the needed sunlight. The former state champion measured 137' in height. Planted in 1917, the trees are now being managed as needed for a continuous healthy hillside forest.

Difficulty Rating 3

1. Norway Spruce

146" CBH   128' VH   48' ACS   Total Points 286   Good Condition
GPS: N 43.630997°   W 072.518137°
Δ State Champion

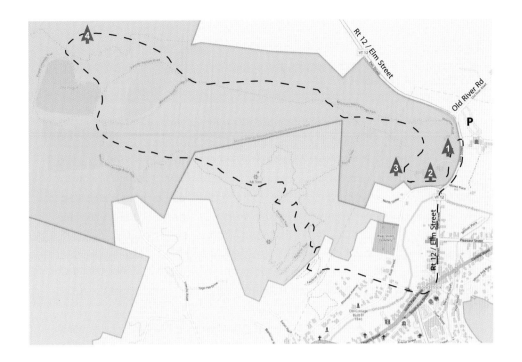

2. White Pine near lower shed

148" CBH   135.5' VH   47' ACS   Total Points 295   Good Condition
GPS: N 43.629729° W 072.520628°

3. White Pine up hill near Cemetery Road

147" CBH   133' VH   53' ACS   Total Points 293   Fair Condition
GPS: N 43.630045° W 072.521517°

4. Hemlock

133" CBH   99' VH   41' ACS   Total Points 242   Fair Condition
GPS: N 43.635177° W 072.541377°

Directions

From the center of Woodstock, take Elm Street (Rt 12) ¼ mile to the end and go right onto Old River Road. Go ¼ mile to the entrance of the Billings Farm and Museum.

Ely Mountain

This trip will bring you through some small towns and back roads near Lake Fairlee onto the side of Ely Mountain. The trees you will see are the largest diameter white ash in the state, along with a nice red pine and some sugar maples, including one named the Spirit Maple. Thetford is among the hills just off the Connecticut River, and there are some very large trees grown in the hills on both sides of the river. You can go through Post Mills on the way and be amazed to see a huge dinosaur made of scrap wood as you go by. Lake Fairlee is a scenic small lake with some summer camps for girls and boys.

The land on Ely Mountain is owned and managed by the Upper Valley Land Trust (UVLT), based in Hanover, NH. This conservation group has worked to set aside an impressive number of properties that allow public access on both sides of the Connecticut River. Landowners in the area who do not want to see their land developed turn to them for help to keep their land as it is and, in the family, with an easement that pays for some or all of the development value. If the owners decide to sell, they have the options of turning to the land trust, which can help raise the money to buy the land. It then can be owned by the land trust, the town, or some other conservation group. The land then can provide access for recreation, a place for wildlife, and keep the rural character of the area intact. There are also unseen benefits, like flood protection from the trees that help absorb rainwater. Land trust organizations like the UVLT play an important part in keeping Vermont and other northern New England states the way we like it, with plenty of open space for people and wildlife.

When I visited, there was no parking area or trails but plans were in the works and now there is a small parking area with trails marked out that will bring you to some of the Big Trees and then on to the top of the mountain. Cross over the brook, and as you start going uphill, keep an eye out for a red pine. This is a nice healthy tree and larger than average for its type. I recently restored a boat built in Norway called a Norwegian skiff that was planked with Norway pine. That is the alternate name for this wood, so I tried to locate some to use when replacing a few planks. It proved difficult on short notice, but red pine lumber is available at times.

Ash with Jason Bedard and Shawn Martin.

It is most often mixed with white pine when sawn and both are sold as pine. Keep going uphill and the trail will bring you to or within sight of the big ash. You will notice that it is hollow enough on the inside to fit a person or two. This is an example of trees that grow to great size in the Connecticut River Valley. There are some impressive oaks of similar size on the NH side of the river.

Although ash is not durable when out in the weather, it is used extensively for things that are used outdoors and then put away under cover when not in use. Snowshoes, baseball bats, sleds, and pack baskets are some examples. In boatbuilding, its bending properties and light weight for its strength make it desirable for steam-bent ribs and stems for small boats that are not moored in the water.

Spirit tree.

Not too much further up the hill, you will come to the sugar maple that has been called the Spirit Tree. The story that has been passed down with the property is that an early owner who was part Native American was given the property by his parents when they passed. His mother had really enjoyed this tree and asked that it not be cut down. At some point, the son had to sell the land and was concerned that the tree could be cut and he would not honor his mother's wishes. Some locals noticed that the tree had been hit by lightning and they told him thinking he would be upset. He said he was relieved though because the lightning had released his mother's spirit from the tree and he could now sell the land with no concerns. Luckily it has ended up in the hands of the UVLT, who I am sure will continue to honor her wishes and respect the property as a whole.

Difficulty rating 3

Ash

195" CBH   87' VH   57' ACS   Total Points 296   Fair Condition
GPS: N 43.87691°   W 072.21664°

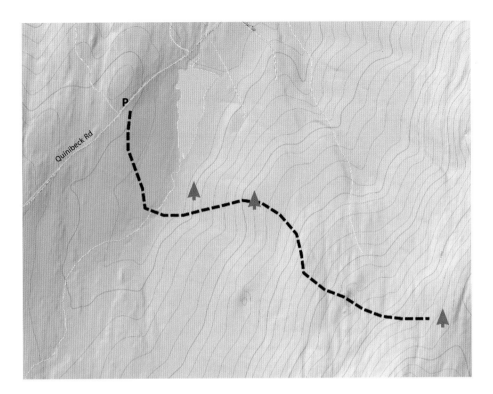

Red Pine

76" CBH   95' VH   30' ACS   Total Points 179   Good Condition
GPS: N 43.87740° W 072.21837°

Spirit Tree

Can't miss it, right on the trail further up the hill.

Directions

From Route 91, take Exit 14 in Thetford. Go left on 113 and follow that through Thetford Center to Post Mills. Turn right on 244 in Post Mills and then right again onto Robinson Hill Road. Follow that past the outlet for Lake Fairlee to Five Corners and take Quinibeck Road a short distance. Look for a sign on the right for Ely Mountain with the Upper Valley Land Trust name on it and the parking area.

Montpelier

There are a few nice trees located in Vermont's capital city that will give you one more reason to visit this impressive place. The other reasons, besides political ones, include the bike path along the Winooski River, strolling past the architecturally impressive buildings, lunch at the many small sandwich shops, and the tower on Hubbard Hill. If you drive around the back roads much, be prepared for the fairly steep hillsides that border the city. The capital building itself is impressive with its massive columns and a statue of Ethan Allen waiting to greet you at the door. The expansive lawns in front of the building allow the public to feel comfortable on the grounds of the statehouse that serves its people. The types of trees you can visit here include an elm, a ginkgo, cottonwood, and hemlock.

You can bike or walk to three of these trees but may have to park your bike and walk to the hemlock. Start by parking at the bike trail lot near the market off Stone Cutters Way. Ride on the bike path toward the center of town; when it comes to Main Street the path peters out and an active RR trestle goes over the North Branch of the Winooski River. To bypass that, you can ride behind the stores along Main Street as far as you can get, then walk the bikes around the corner going left on State Street and past the storefronts there. As you come to some areas with access to parking lots behind a church, ride into these parking areas picking up the bike path again along the railroad tracks and the river. The bike path goes along the river, across Route 2, and behind the high school. Continue along there until you come to the Peace Park and your first tree, a cottonwood. There are many other larger cottonwoods in Vermont, but this is a fairly good-sized one and in a nice park where you can stop at and enjoy the river a minute. This particular tree has a hole in the bottom on the river side, and I would imagine it is home to some water-loving mammal like a river otter or mink.

When ready, head back the way you came to the center of town, and after crossing the pedestrian bridge, catch Taylor Street up to and across State Street to Governor Davis Avenue, which ends at Court Street. With the corner of the capitol building to the left, look to the right and you will see the stately American elm. At 150", it is not the

Ginkgo.

biggest elm, but this is one of Montpelier's largest trees. Dutch elm disease wiped out most of this type of tree across the state, but some were isolated or resistant survivors like this one. The lumber has been used for many things in the past, including water pipes and gutters on houses.

From the elm, we walked up to Hubbard Tower on a path with slate stairways starting at the end of Court Street near the statehouse. I am going to suggest another way that takes you around the hill to the back of the park where the hemlock is. That way you can walk the tower loop instead of up to the tower and down to the tree on the other side, then back up to the tower and down to the town again. To get to the other side of the hill, go to the other end of Court Street and take a left onto Elm

Street, then a left on Spring Street, then left again onto Parkway Avenue. Follow that and bear left toward the top and the second parking area. Take the tower loop trail up to the tower and be sure to go up it to see Camels Hump, a famously shaped mountaintop you can view in the distance. Then go down, continuing the loop and working your way to the seven fireplaces picnic area and the unusual outhouse with a view. The hemlock here is good-sized considering that this whole hill was pasture only one hundred years ago. This and some others have the old-growth bark on them and likely were some of the few conifers not cut when the pasture was made. After checking the hemlock, make your way back on the tower trail to Parkway Avenue and take the big pine trail around to see them and go right on the fitness trail to make a loop back to the parking area.

To finish the tour of Montpelier, go back down Parkway to Main Street and either go through town to Barre Street or work your way there on back roads to avoid traffic in town. Go on Barre Street to the CPA offices at #143 and the second-largest ginkgo tree in Vermont. The ginkgo biloba, also called the maidenhair tree, is one of the oldest living tree species. Fossils of the leaves from 65 million years ago are identical to today's leaves. Native to China, the leaf and seed of this species has been used for medicine for thousands of years and its use continues on around the world today. An extract from the dried green leaves is used in the west to treat dementia, anxiety, glaucoma and other eye diseases, to improve memory and thinking. The Chinese and others in Asia have used the seeds for similar medicinal benefits. Fothergill, Segale, and Valley is the accounting firm based here and they take pride in the tree and the grounds it is on. Be sure to stay on the sidewalk as you take a good look at this amazing medical wonder with its fan-shaped leaves. When ready, go on to Granite Street and the parking area where you started out.

Difficulty Rating 2

1. Cottonwood

Not big for cottonwood.
No measurements. Just go for the bike ride and visit Peace Park.

2. American Elm

150" CBH   77' VH   77' ACS   Total Points   246   Good Condition
GPS: N 44.262093°   W 72.578390°

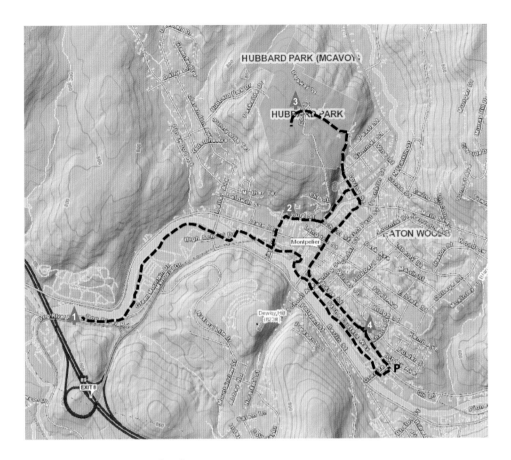

3. Eastern Hemlock

102" CBH   88' VH   53' ACS   Total Points 203   Good Condition
No GPS. Just look for biggest hemlocks while on Tower Loop Trail

4. Ginkgo

210" CBH   65' VH   53' ACS   Total Points 278   Good Condition
GPS: N 44.255465°   W 72.572601°

Directions

Get off I-89 in Montpelier and take Memorial Drive. Go left on Route 12
and just over the bridge go right onto Stonecutters Way and find parking
about ¼ mile down near the bike trail.

Burlington

Burlington is the best city in Vermont for a bike tour of Big Trees. There are bike paths that bring you along the waterfront and you can continue through back roads and cemeteries to where the Big Trees are. The beaches and parks along Lake Champlain are bound to impress. It has a great downtown area with many shops and restaurants. You can walk or bike through town to the Church Street shopping plaza, have lunch at a French restaurant, then hit the Outdoor Gear Exchange to get your hiking gear fix.

After a few visits to Burlington, it has grown on me as a city that highlights Vermont as a Mecca for the outdoor enthusiasts. It is one of the most bike friendly places I have seen, and with Lake Champlain and the nearby mountains, there is plenty of outdoor activity to be had. There are not many viewable trees in the downtown area, but if you make your way to the Lakeview Cemetery, that will make up for the lack of trees in town.

One visit had us starting at the southern end at Oakledge Park, then pedaling through town past North Beach and the cemetery. The next visit had us biking from Leddy Park to Colchester, then over the

Church Street in the morning.

Impressive red oak at the Lakeview Cemetery. ▶

causeway across the lake to the bike ferry that brings you to South Hero on Grand Isle.

If you want to make a day of it, start biking at the southern end of town by leaving your car at one of the parks or find a roadside spot near there. Catch the bike path at the park and ride along the lake. The path leaves the waterfront and goes up to and beside an active railroad track, then back past the waterfront into the city. You will have passed a few large cottonwoods and maples along the way, and you may see a few more cottonwoods off in the distance. Now may be when you can spend some time walking or biking through downtown to see the sights, shop, and eat, or wait until on your way back, depending on your timing.

There will be plenty of spots along the bike trail to take breaks if needed. After the downtown area, you can follow the path up past the fenced-in side of the cemetery to North Beach Park and get off the bike path at the park entrance. Get on Institute Road past the high school, pedaling up to North Avenue and heading back south or right to the Lakeview Cemetery. The cemetery is owned and managed by the City of Burlington. Maps of the trees on the grounds, made by Branch Out Burlington, along with other info, is available online. Go in the main entrance and work your way toward the lake while looking out for the trees listed here.

In the middle, you will find the hemlock at the central monument and bench area. At 126" in circumference, this is fairly large compared to most I have seen in Vermont and could have been a champ if the top had not been blown off. It seems many of the trees here are short in height due to the heavy winds off the lake causing damage to the topmost branches. Most of them being open-grown means they tend to spread out instead of up, which is another factor influencing their short stature. In my area of NH, hemlock is the choice local wood for rafters and floor joists. While not as good as spruce for strength and ability to hold fastenings, it is stronger than pine, and the more northern-grown spruce is not available at the small local mills. This tree has marks on the bark and I noticed a nest in the top. The gray squirrels have chosen this hemlock for their nest site and go up and down and chase each other around on its trunk.

Keep heading toward the southern edge of the cemetery with an eye out for the largest circumference Norway spruce. This will be tough because there are so many large ones spread around, but you will find it if you keep looking. This one is not as nice-looking as some of the others, but it has character and the roots are large and crawl around to the gravestones, seeming to draw life from the souls buried nearby.

A white oak is not far off that is surely worth a look. The bark is falling off on one side, but from a distance the crown looks healthy. It may be hollow and if the bark falls off all the way around it will likely die. I would say it is in fair condition. What do you think? Sometimes it is hard to decide, maybe poor but not good or excellent condition.

After deciding on the condition of the white oak, continue on down near the lake and you will find a tree that I would say is in excellent condition. It's such a nice tree, I cannot bear to give it less. Although some might say good condition because the crown is not perfectly symmetrical or some branches may have been trimmed or fallen, when you are done looking at it, this tree will stick in your mind as a most impressive and excellent example of a red oak. I will have to associate this tree with whitetail deer, as three young ones appeared and were looking for a handout while there on one trip. This species is the most common hardwood in southern parts of the Northeast and is very important as a mast crop, with acorns that all sorts of wildlife depend on. In northern Vermont, red oak is likely not as common as some of your other hardwoods such as yellow birch or beech. This particular tree fits right in as a highlight to end your visit to this outstanding destination city in northern Vermont.

Difficulty Rating 1

1. Eastern Hemlock

126" CBH   75' VH   54' ACS   Total Points   215   Excellent Condition
GPS: N 44.492096°   W 73.231771°

2. White Oak

181" CBH   72' VH   82' ACS   Total Points 273   Fair Condition
GPS: N 44.490883°   W 73.232365°

3. Norway Spruce

145" CBH   76' VH   51' ACS   Total Points 234   Good Condition
GPS: N 44.491270°   W 73.232101°

4. Red Oak

216" CBH   76' VH   83' ACS   Total Points 312   Excellent Condition
GPS: N 44.49279°   W 073.23222°

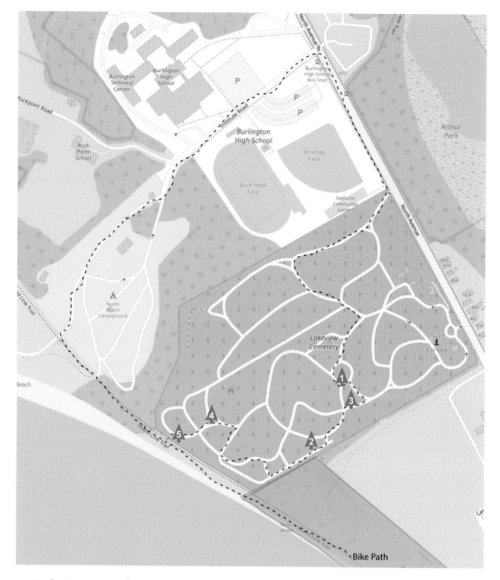

Bike Path

5. Cottonwood

179" CBH   101' VH   69' ACS   Total Points 297   Good Condition
GPS: N 44.49033°   W 073.23376°

Directions

From I-89, get off on Route 7 North in Burlington. Go about a ½ mile and take a left onto Flynn Avenue. Follow it to the end for parking at Oakledge Park. About a 4-mile bike ride, so 8 miles round trip. If walking, you can drive right to the Lakeview Cemetery on North Ave in Burlington.

Eastern Cottonwood *[Populus deltoids]*

This tree is known for its height in many areas and grows best in Vermont along the floodplains of larger rivers and lakeshores. The cottonwood seeds are dispersed in cotton-like strands that float through the air, then settle in the flooded rivers to be carried downstream to another site with the right soil for growth of a new tree. A fast-growing tree that can reach 11' in diameter will sprout up along the river wherever the conditions are right. If you walk along the river at the right time of year, it will seem like the air is filled with cotton. The lumber was used at one time for house and barn construction in the Midwest because it was readily available. A few woodsmen were known to have lived in hollow standing cottonwoods. Logs of great size were also burned out by Native Americans and then carved into dugout canoes when needed. I imagine that the hollow trunk of some of the old trees would be almost ready for use with only a little burning and tool work needed. The light, fuzzy wood is not currently sought after for furniture but is used for pallets and crates.

Woodside Natural Area is the perfect place to see the cottonwoods in a setting that is typical for these trees. The trail goes along the midsize Woonoski River, allowing you to see the floodplains and associated wetlands. Take the Loop Trail to the left and you will pass some smaller cottonwoods and the green ash that often grows along with them. The trail takes you up along a ridge near the Juvenile Rehabilitation Center, and from there you go around a wetland where three blue herons flew out of as we walked by. As you meet the Fern Trail, there are some impressive trees that are in a real nice setting near the river, but if you keep going on the Loop Trail, the biggest will show up soon. Be careful around the trees and stay on the trails, especially in mid-summer. The stinging nettles are of great size here, and you'll learn how they got their name if you brush up against them. I felt the numbing sting a few times while measuring here.

What is important to take note of is the height of these trees, with the two I measured at 130' and 140'. Known to grow at a rate of five or six feet in height per year when saplings, these tall examples are likely not very old. The distinct bark is similar to but coarser than the closely related aspens, which are also fast growers.

Tall cottonwood.

Difficulty Rating 2

126" CBH   140' VH   76' ACS   Total Points 285   Excellent Condition
GPS: N 44.50083°   W 073.14188°

116" CBH   130' VH   53.5' ACS   Total Points 259   Excellent Condition
GPS: N 44.50153°   W 073.13876°

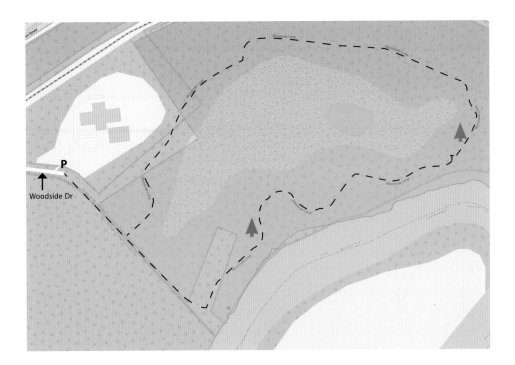

Directions

Coming out of the Burlington area on I-89 N, take Route 15 in Winooski east toward Essex. Go 1.3 mile and look for Ethan Allen College on the left, and you can take a right at the lights opposite the Barnes Avenue entrance road to the school. The right is Woodside Drive. Follow it and bear right down near the Juvenile Rehabilitation Center and the gate for the Woodside Trail.

Shelburne Bay Park

This park is outstanding for its many pockets of different types of trees. The trail here follows along the Shelburne Bay shore and goes up Allen Hill, looping through old hemlock and pines, then past some big burr and white oaks, into small groups of eastern hophornbeam, northern white cedar, red cedar, and chestnut oaks. Its location just outside of Burlington draws many visitors, so you will have company most days while on a walk here, but as you get up near Allen Hill the trail gets narrow and less used. I particularly liked the side of the hill near the lake withs its cedar shores and a ledge outcrop with a jaw-dropping view across the bay.

The Clark Trail starts off as wide and gravel road near the back parking lot. You go past Zoey's Landing, as says the sign on a cedar tree, a sloping rock ledge that gently goes into the bay, looking perfect for pulling a canoe or small boat to shore. Not long into it, you will see a few

Biggest burr oak.

View from the ledge.

big oaks hovering out of the wood line over the water to the right of the trail. I measured one of those burr oaks and thought it an outstanding start, with a mature tree found rather quickly. I spent some time looking for acorns and taking leaf photos so I could determine the type of oak.

Further along and inland a bit, a similar oak shows up right on the trail as you start up the hill. This is a bit bigger and taller than the shoreline tree. Head up the hill and past the junction where the Clark Trail loops back and get on the Allen Hill Trail going over the ridge and into a wetter pocket with the eastern hophornbeam spread all around. I had read something about a large one on the property, and the biggest I saw measured about 50" around. Being forked, it was rather short so I did not measure it fully. Keep an eye out for it right next to the trail. You will see more of them on the other side of the hill, too. Just past the hophornbeam it turns into a white cedar woods, with its completely different look and feel. Snowshoeing in the winter through this would be great, and you are likely to have the close company of chickadees and other small birds seeking their shelter and food. Eventually, some red cedar starts to mix in and dominate, which I thought a bit unusual seeing the two types of cedar together. As you round the end to the shoreline, the white cedar comes back heavy and makes for a great shoreline presence. As you loop back along the shore heading up higher, do not miss the lookout ledge high above the bay with its views down to the water and across to the colorful hills, if you make a fall visit. It gets a bit steeper for a while as you head to the top of the hill past more hophornbeam, until it gets level and you start down past the chestnut oak with its deeply fissured bark dominating the hillside.

Once you come to the Clark Trail, follow it back on the inland part of the loop. Most of the forest is young there, having been cut over recently, but it's a different look and you go through some pine and hemlocks. I ended up back at the landing and out to the parking lot where I noticed a shrub-covered oak trunk in the grassy opening that begged me to measure it. It turned out to be the biggest tree in the Shelburne Bay Park. While these burr oaks are big enough to impress this NH native, states like Ohio routinely measure this species in the 200"–250"-circumference range. There appears to be a bit different climate along the Vermont side of Champlain, so there are some more southerly trees doing well here, while it's still cold enough for the northerly trees to thrive too. As I was driving to the area from NH in late October, the foliage was gone much of the way here, but when I arrived the colors of the leaves were still showing when drawing near the lake.

As for a wildlife connection, I would connect the spot to waterfowl of many types and possibly eagles that may roost here. I did notice large bird remains near the paths where I imagine an eagle or maybe a hawk made a meal of the ducks they caught and then brought to the shore to eat. All in all, a great place to visit with mature trees and a great variety that is sure to educate you in some way.

Difficulty Rating 3

Burr Oak by lakeshore

120" CBH   60' VH   47' ACS   Total Points 192   Good Condition
GPS: N 44.405521°   W 073.239064°

Burr Oak on hillside

136" CBH   83' VH   No ACS.   Good Condition
GPS: N 44.405573°   W 073.239027°

Burr Oak in parking area

181" CBH   62.5' VH   67' ACS   Total Points 260   Fair Condition
GPS: N 44.400202°   W 073.236927°

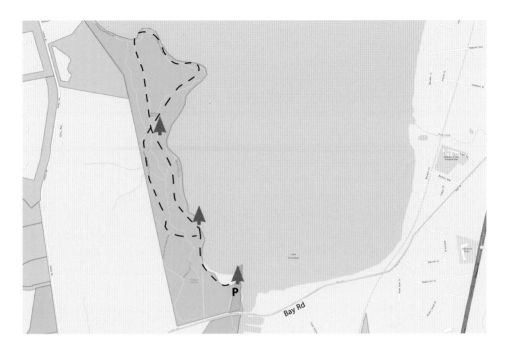

Directions

From I-89 in Burlington, take 189 W to Route 7. Go south about 2.7 miles and take a right onto Bay Road and go 1.2 miles to Shelburne Bay. Park on the right.

Williams Woods Natural Area Oaks

This natural area is one of the fifty-eight natural areas conserved and managed by the Nature Conservancy in Vermont. The lands they have protected are some of the best natural communities in the state, and Williams Woods is a prime example. A map and property description is available to download on their website. This land is described as one of the best remaining stands of mature valley clayplain forest in the Champlain Valley. This type of forest and its mature trees provides a different and important habitat for many wildlife species with its hollow, fallen oak logs that rot from the center out.

The trail starts from the road, and it's a bit wet in areas, but the

Biggest swamp white oak.

boardwalks are abundant and keep your feet dry. The first trees worthy of noting are a few mature, straight and tall red maples. It's been difficult to find real big red maples in a wooded setting to have as a highlighted tree that we can visit. The real big ones I have measured were in cemeteries and street sides. I think they must eventually get shaded out and die before getting very big in the woods. Many of the older growth trees like these have bark that starts breaking off into long plates similar to shagbark hickory. Continuing on the trail, a large oak will draw your attention over near the cornfields. The extra sunlight is shaping it into a tall-trunked, mature tree soon to be a champion. A little further on is another that is even bigger in circumference. As a boatbuilder, I was drooling with thoughts of how much long clear lumber would come from prime trees like these that could be used for keels of wooden boats, but I realize they are better served here as ambassadors for helping people appreciate the forests. Some other lands can be managed for the occasional cutting of the good-sized oaks while they are still prime lumber trees and don't start to hollow out too much. This property has many of these mature but not-too-old trees of the white oak family that have long straight trunks.

As you move along the loop trail, there are some older growth hemlocks and pines mixed in then you go through quite a bit of younger new growth pines leaving you to wonder when the big trees will show up. Then, suddenly, a great swamp white oak shows itself at the edge of the wetland next to Thorpe Brook. This is a wildlife haven, with many mammals and waterfowl likely eating the acorns and the beaver chewing a nearby tree and avoiding this large, too-tough-to-handle oak. I would have to associate this tree with the beaver, as it often grows where they are active creating their own wildlife haven by backing up the water providing a home for many plants and a feeding area for ducks, deer, and other wildlife. With this and other trees on sloping or wet grounds, be sure to stay a bit away from the trunk to take your photos and try to take care to prevent tamping down or eroding the soil here. Although there is a larger one recorded in Vermont, this is one of the largest I have measured, and you can appreciate it more in this setting. The loop continues around through the young woods, then you gradually see more of those outstanding mature oaks that make you stop and admire them as you head back to your car.

Swamp white oak top.

Difficulty Rating 2

Swamp White Oak

144" CBH   72' VH   62' ACS   Total Points 231   Excellent Condition
GPS: N 44.273106°   W 073.256104°

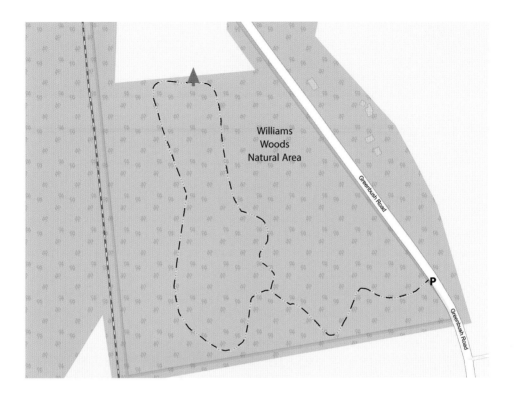

Directions

Take Route 7 South from Burlington. In Charlotte, go right on Ferry Road at the lights, Go 0.3 miles and take left onto Greenbush Road. Go 2 miles and veer left at a corner, staying on Greenbush, which then goes right at a tricky fork in the road. Go 1 mile further on Greenbush and look for the Williams Woods sign on the right, with parking on the side of the road.

Cambridge Pines

The towering pines in the Cambridge Pines Woods are worth checking out because of their height, and it's one of the top big pine areas in the state. We stayed in Stowe and chose to come through Smugglers Notch to see the trees here, adding to the appeal of the trip. Be aware that the road through the notch narrows to one lane and twists and turns around house-sized boulders near the top. You have to step on the gas all the way up and hope no car comes down the other way as you go around the boulders. Not for the faint of heart. This road closes for the winter. If coming up from NH on I-93 or VT on I-91, you can get on the Grand Army of the Republic Highway and get to Cambridge without going through the notch.

Sally Laughlin and pines.

The best access is through the newly conserved Peter A. Krusch Nature Preserve, which is off North Cambridge Road. The preserve was the vision of the longtime landowner Peter Krusch, who wanted the land set aside for the public. His widow, Sally Laughlin followed through, by working with the Vermont Land Trust and the town of Cambridge to preserve the land and make the trails and stream crossings for your use.

The trail starts going up from the parking lot into a small pasture that will be kept open for birds and other wildlife that needs that kind of habitat. It heads back into the woods on an easy-going new path that brings you to the first bridge over Dragon Brook, named for its roaring sound when the spring freshets fill it with water. The name also gives a hint to Peter's former profession of making metal art sculptures in the form of dragons. The woods themselves have many types of trees, including some that are starting to get large and old. A few pines were over 100" circumference, and there are some maples a little bigger, showing the shaggy bark of a mature red maple. Sally has hopes that the trees will become attractions that enhance the Cambridge Pines experience in future years. Jonathan Woods, the forester for the preserve, suggests that the best management plan is to allow the trees to grow naturally to large size with little or no cutting or thinning required. After crossing another bridge, you will see a sign telling you the pine forest is ahead. There are no trails here at this time, and I am not sure that they are planned, so you will have to go it on your own and use your map and compass or GPS to get around. At about twenty-two acres, the property is not too big, and besides climbing over a few massive fallen trunks, the only issue may be the steep slopes of two ravines that cut through the forest.

Start along the boundary of the open pasture land and go to the pine that Sally showed me as a larger one here. It's on a slope and big indeed, so it will get your interest going. Keep going down on an angle over the first ravine, then back up the other side. Heading through the heart of the woods, there are many pines over 3' diameter spread throughout and some blown-over trees that require some effort to get over. I think this adds to the appeal of these woods, giving you an idea how old-growth pit and mound forests get started. Follow a faint wildlife trail angling down the next ravine and look across and up to what is a clearing where the cemetery is located. Three-quarters of the way up, you will notice a very large and tall pine. This is the largest measured here and quite impressive with its 4'-plus-diameter trunk and 140' VH. I measured another nearby in 2014 of a similar size and height on the back side of the cemetery not too far away. I did not see it when I visited, but I've heard of another that is supposed to be even bigger in circumference on the slope up behind the house near the entrance to the cemetery. A hemlock has also been reported at 154" C. These white pines were set aside in the 1940s and are up to two hundred years old.

Lumber from the pine tree is used in boatbuilding as planking in small, dory-style boats and decking in large boats. I have used quarter-sawn pine, cut to 3/16" in thickness, for planks in lightweight Adirondack guideboats that are popular in up-state NY. Trees of this size were also set aside in coastal areas of New England for use on colonial British boats as ships masts. There were some notable skirmishes between the British and Americans over the cutting of these trees.

Wildlife seen here included a hawk that would appreciate these pines for roosting and thrushes that depend on the mixed hardwoods also found in this area.

Difficulty Rating 3 Off trail. Steep slopes. Might need GPS.

Pine at back of cemetery—could be same tree as below.

154" CBH   144 VH   44'ACS   Total Points 309 (2013)   Good Condition
GPS: N 44.65306°   W 072.87706°

Pine by cemetery measured in 2021.

164" CBH   140' VH   42' ACS   Total Points 314 (2021)   Good Condition
GPS: N 44.653211°   W 072.876171°
Δ Tied for State Champion

Sally's Pine

149" CBH   127' VH   47' ACS   Total Points 287 (2021)   Good Condition
GPS: N 44.654691°   W 072.877368°

Directions

From the Grand Army of the Republic Highway or Route 15, take Pumpkin Harbor Road near the bridge in Cambridge, then go about 1 mile to a right onto North Cambridge Road. Take that about a ¼ mile and, just past Krusch Drive, look for the parking area on the right.

Old-Growth Trees

There has been much discussion over the years on what constitutes an old-growth forest or an old-growth tree. It's important to separate the two descriptions. Old-growth forests have many features in the landscape besides the trees themselves that determines if it is an actual old forest. There must be pits and mounds on the forest floor where generations of trees have toppled over and the pulled-up roots have created the pits, as well as the stumps and logs that create the mounds after the fallen trees have all but disappeared. Most of the large-growing trees must be at least 150 years old with no sign of human interference or fires opening the land.

The old-growth trees, on the other hand, can be found in many places where there has been human involvement and new younger trees are growing all around. It may be a boundary tree or in a small plot with a few other large older trees but minus the topography of an old-growth forest. Black gum woods come to mind as a bit different, too. They are mostly old trees and can grow together in areas, but because the gums were not a desired tree to cut, many of the other types of trees nearby were harvested around them, leaving the gums as old trees but not an old forest.

Some old-growth forests will have old trees that are not of the great size we look for while searching for Big Trees. Hemlocks will stay in the shade of other trees for hundreds of years waiting to gain size when an opening is created when a larger nearby pine or oak dies or is blown over. These older trees have their own appeal, though, with their craggy bark and that deep-forest feel in many spots when you find them bunched together. Once you get your expectations in order, I'm sure you will appreciate visits to these trees even if they are not the giants of the woods.

Red Pine *[Pinus resinosa]*

This part of the Northeast Kingdom is quite impressive in the fall, with many small tree-covered mountains and a wilderness feel to it, with the Clyde and Nulhegan rivers running along route 105. Island Pond is a perfectly situated small town within all this countryside, with its namesake lake right nearby. Brighton State Park is next door in Brighton, and it has groves of naturally grown red pine that are bound to impress those who know this type of tree. While they are quite common in the Midwest, most of what we see in New England are the quaint rows that were, and still are, often planted in areas that have been clear cut and where the owners want a fast replacement crop

Ross Stevens and red pine.

Natural red pine woods.

of trees that may give them some return in their lifetime. The natural groves commonly grew in after fires, and that is what happened here over one hundred years ago. In 1853, the railroad came to town and along with it the logging industry. As many as five hundred loggers once worked the area. After the cutting, a fire came through in 1903 burning as much as 1,200 acres.

Spectacle Pond is a small pond with history going back to before European settlers. Once known as Old Man's Nose, the point of land on the northern part of the pond is now known as Indian Point. Native American tribes used the point as a meeting ground, and the champion wrestler Don Eagle's father, Chief War Eagle, once lived here. They sold the land to the state of Vermont in the 1950s so it could become the park you are now enjoying.

Ross Stevens from the Northwoods Stewardship Center in nearby Charlestown guided us to the tree. The organization has the mission of connecting people and places through science education and action. The center itself is a destination for young people interested in forestry and our natural resources. It sits on 1,500 acres with a conference center, classrooms, and a woodworking shop. There are also trails and campsites on the property. They work with the Conservation Corp and many other organizations to bring attention to the forests and their importance to the region.

The state park has several walking trails to enjoy here, and you can pay the fee and start from the park in season or take a canoe like we did and enjoy a paddle to see Indian Point and the unusual sight of a full grove of red pines from the water. If canoeing, you can start at the boat launch on Fishing Village Road off Lakeshore Drive near 105. There is no boat launch at the state park, but you can rent a rowboat or kayak there. It is a short paddle to the point at the other side, which can be seen straight across from the launch. As you paddle up, be sure to get a good look at Indian Point and pull in the cove to the right or NE. The Northern Forest Canoe Trail comes through here, and there is a sign and sandy landing enticing you to pull up and get out. Leave some room in case another canoeist comes along and then check out Indian Point before taking the Shore Trail on the right. Before the logging and fires, this area was once covered by ancient white pines and considered a peaceful spot for council fires and talks by the natives of the area. Even now it seems very peaceful and a special spot to relax.

To see the state champion red pine, continue on the shore trail, and, before long, you will see another trail coming in on the left. Follow that and you shortly come to the tree. If you have seen other red pines, you will know this is of a size rarely seen around this part of the country. It is tall, at 103', and any of these close to 100" in circumference is large for its type. This pine can be ID'd by its distinctive flakey, reddish bark and the fact that the needles come in pairs of two. Scotch pine also has two, but the bark turns orange near the top, so you can easily tell the difference. Pitch pine has three needles and white pine has five.

You may notice this pine has many dead lower branches, and the fact that these types of trees will self-prune helps it become one of the most fire-resistant species. The ground fires will not reach up to the higher branches, and the layered bark protects the lower trunk. The heat from the fire then opens the cones to release the seeds into the prime growing conditions left below. The fact that trunks of these pines do not taper much toward the top makes them ideal for use as telephone poles when

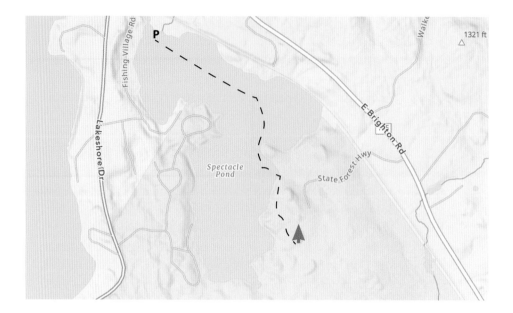

treated, and many poles along the roads are of this type of tree. Other uses of the lumber are described in a previous chapter. Many insects feed on the red pine's needles, cones, and bark, while several birds and small mammals eat those insects and the seeds. When I paddled over here, a mother loon and its adolescent young were right near the point. I will associate them with the red pines, as their calls just seemed to suit the spot.

Difficulty Rating 2

96" CBH   103' VH   42.5' ACS   Total Points 210   Good Condition
GPS: N 44.796882°   W 71.847496°; or N 44.797061°   W 71.847244°.
Δ State Champion and competitor for National Champion

Directions

To get to Brighton State Park, follow Route 105 from Newport and I-91 to the town of Island Pond. You will see a sign for Brighton State Park just as you get into the outskirts of the town. Take that right on Pleasant Street, then a left on Lakeshore Drive to the entrance of Brighton State Park. You can pull in there and hike the trails and rent a canoe if you like. The other option is to go past the entrance and take the last right off Lakeshore Drive onto Fishing Village Road past the camps to the boat launch. From here you will have to paddle out to the tree.

About the Author

Kevin Martin has been interested in working with wood all of his adult life, brought on by exposure to his father's collection of wood-working tools and using the wooden boat that his father built. Early on he put in a four-year apprenticeship as a union carpenter before starting his own business, Kevin Martin Wooden Boats and Canoes [https://kevinmartin.wcha.org/]. For over 40 years Kevin has carried on the tradition of boatbuilding, constructing well over one hundred small crafts and restoring many more. A visit to his workshop will usually include seeing at least one or two fascinating canoes or boats in progress.

His interest in working with wood led him to admire the giant trees he came across in the woods of New Hampshire. At first, he looked at them as prime sources of good lumber for his work. After serving many years on the town Conservation Commission, and then the Lamprey River Advisory Committee he learned of their many other important benefits.

Kevin's interest in Big Trees began when searching for some trees he had heard about in wildlife studies that were completed along the Lamprey River. He found some state champions in special natural settings that brought about a great respect for the different types of forests found in New Hampshire. This led to his work as a volunteer for the NH Big Tree Program where he was the state coordinator and Rockingham County coordinator while training as a member of the National Big Tree measuring group. He published his first book *Big Trees of New Hampshire (Peter E. Randall Publisher)* in 2014 and then traveled Northern New England for seven years to produce the current book.

Kevin and his wife, Kim, have raised a family of four children in the house that they built in Epping on the banks of the Lamprey River. They have 8 grandchildren and the family will at times go along with him in the woods. He is an accomplished naturalist and outdoorsman, and shares many of his experiences in this book the *Big Trees of Northern New England*.

Index by Tree Type